D0513502

Strictly Come Dancing

The Official 2012 Annual

Alison Maloney

BBC
BOOKS

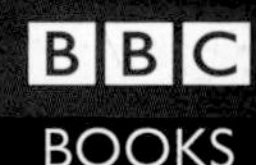

Contents

THE JUDGES VOTE

EXCLUSIVE FEATURES

THE STRICTLY NIGHT IN

A few words from Sir Bruce Forsyth

In my opinion, last year's *Strictly Come Dancing* contained some of the best dances and the funniest moments we've ever had. It was a wonderful series with a nail-biting final in which Kara Tointon was a very worthy winner. To be honest, I didn't know her before the show because I don't watch soap operas at all but I was thrilled to see that she went straight from *Strictly* into the West End to play the lead role in *Pygmalion*.

During the run, I asked her to do a gag with me. The newspapers were saying that she was 'drop dead gorgeous' so after she finished her dance I said to her 'I think you're gorgeous' and she said 'drop dead!'. It got a big laugh because she delivered the line so well and I was more than impressed. Now she's a West End star and a great dancer who can turn her hand, and her feet, to anything; she's a lovely girl and deserves a fantastic career.

Competition to lift the trophy last year was particularly tough because the final three – Kara, Matt and Pamela – all turned into great dancers before our very eyes and I hope the public realise how hard they worked to achieve that.

It was also a year when our more mature ladies were a big hit. Felicity Kendal brought her Tinkerbell personality into her dancing and Pamela Stephenson was phenomenal, so graceful and elegant. She loved doing the show because she got her sylph like figure back. It was an amazing transformation. And then, of course, there was Ann Widdecombe our best comedy act ever. She was absolutely wonderful and I was so thrilled when they put her with Anton; they were made for each other! They were the novelty act of the series and every week I looked forward to seeing what they were getting up to, as did the viewers. I'll never forget the moment she flew down from the rafters! The reaction from the studio audience was incredible, she had such fun and threw herself into it – literally! Anton was receiving food parcels every day to keep his strength up but Ann was a revelation. Any of you who saw the *Strictly* tour will have seen Ann dancing with Craig Revell Horwood. Yes!! I'm not kidding!! I've got to get a copy.

We had some fabulous dancers and I hope we can keep up the standard this year. To date, the bar has been raised each year and I'm touching wood at this very moment. The last series got exceptional ratings and it deserved to because it is a show which caters for a very wide audience from young to old. In my mind the show just keeps getting better and better.

Last year we also benefitted from a new set. I thought is this going to work? But it really did. It looked very good on the screen and the big screens meant they were able to do a lot more in terms of special effects so production-wise it was a success. I couldn't be happier for the whole team.

Using props sometimes during the dances was another good innovation which added to the entertainment value. The stage crew coped well with them because they have to act very quickly. They only have a few seconds to whip these things onto the floor because it is a live show, which sometimes people forget. The props are put in place while Tess is up in her golden penthouse chatting to everyone who ventures in there (and as we know she is never lost for words, bless her) so all hail to the stage crew who do such a wonderful job. The whole team on the show are magnificent. Everybody works so hard. How it all fits together I'll never know, but it just works.

Another change for the better, in my view, was scrapping the dance off, which made the results show quicker and better. I'm all for keeping things sharper and I did feel sorry for the couples sometimes when they had to do a dance off. It was almost like a penalty shoot out. It was always a bit hard on them and I don't think it is necessary. We've already seen the dances so why do them again?

Since the end of the last series, I have been honoured with a knighthood and I want to take this opportunity to thank all the *Strictly* fans for their good wishes. I haven't got used to my new title yet but the number of people I've heard from has been amazing. In fact, it's a full-time job thanking everybody for their good wishes.

With the ninth series coming up, I'm as excited as I am every year and thank goodness that this time I haven't had too many people saying 'Is this your last series?' They've been asking me that since the first series eight years ago, so it's become a bit of an old joke. But never mind all that, Keeeeeep Dancing!

Tess Talk

What a treat last year's *Strictly* was for me, with the addition of a brand-new and exciting elevated area overlooking the action on the dance floor. It was fabulous.

My old backstage area was small but it was very comfortable and cosy. It was great in its own way because it was so intimate the couples tended to open up to me. But I'm happy to swap it for my glamorous new home.

Up in my new area, I got to see the dancing on the floor as it happened which was great for the celebs and their professionals, because they could peer over to watch other couples dancing and there was a real sense of team spirit. Also, we could see the audience reaction, watch their faces as they reacted to the dancing, and it added a whole new level of excitement.

The whole set benefitted from the makeover. It looked glamorous, fabulous and exciting and the Hallowe'en special took us into uncharted territory. We got a lot of positive feedback. The audience really enjoyed the use of props and screens – the lapping flames and lightning effects – and it just looked fantastic so I'm hoping for more of that this year.

As a Hollywood actor, Jimi Mistry really threw himself into his character for his *Thriller* paso doble. In fact, he got so into character it was actually quite scary. I loved Jimi, and he was the one, along with Scott, who was shouting, cheering and really pushing the team spirit all the way through. They were team leaders and best mates right up until the point Jimi left, which was far too soon.

I thought the last season had a genius line-up and a great cast of characters. Ann Widdecombe was hysterical. We knew she was outspoken so there wouldn't be a dull moment, but who'd have thought a former Conservative MP could capture the nation's imagination to that degree? When she flew through the air at the start of the tango, it was the funniest thing I'd seen in *Strictly's* history. It was television gold!

Pamela Stephenson was another personal highlight for me. I thought she was wonderful. She completely embraced the show, she was so fearless that even James Jordan was flabbergasted by her stamina. He joked that he was struggling to keep up with her. She talks now about how she benefitted from the entire *Strictly* experience, how she felt more like her old self, she got fitter and she felt all sexy because she got into shape. She enjoyed every moment on the show.

Felicity was incredible, with her splits and her back bends. What a cast! The atmosphere in my area upstairs was electric; it was a joy to be part of it all because there was a real contagious buzz. It swept the nation.

Gavin's guns were very impressive but I felt for him every week. We were just desperate for him to come out of his shell because, despite the fake tan and the posturing in the mirror, he's actually incredibly shy. As a sportsman he's not used to being in the spotlight – the rugby pitch is his home not the dance floor. By his own admission, he got really into it but you could see exactly what he was going through, emotionally. I admired him for putting himself out there, which took real courage.

We were all sad when we lost Tina O'Brien. She and Jared were a dynamite team and all the kids at my daughter's school loved them. They were so cute, but I felt Tina never got the chance to regain her momentum after she had a week off for chicken pox, which was a real shame because she was a darling to watch.

To be honest, for me, the frontrunner was always Kara. I'd seen her dance before in the Sport Relief special where they learnt the routine in a day, and I could see she was a natural mover and was incredibly talented. There was a lot of waterworks because for her it was a very emotional journey but she really blossomed, she found her dancing feet and in the final she blew everybody away.

Kara was really upset when she hurt her arm in the final. She was devastated, and shaking like a leaf. She came up to me, wondering if she could still dance and she was trying desperately not to break down, and Artem was supporting her. I really felt for her because she really did hurt herself. But it was live on the show, it was the final, and every dance every week was all about this moment. She had to pull it off and the professional in her rose to the challenge, and she did just that. She danced through the pain and she was spectacular.

The public vote worked really well because the final three were genuinely the best three dancers and you could have predicted they would be there because they proved themselves all the way through.

After the last few seasons, it was a bonus to have three couples in the final. In the past few years we've had dramas, we've had injuries, people have pulled out of the competition and left us one finalist down. This time we had a full house and it was great to see them go head to head. It was difficult to pick the winner, right down to the show dance. It had us all on the edge of our seats.

Kara's show dance was spectacular and her American smooth was flawless. She looked like a classic Hollywood movie star, so beautiful. Artem, let's not forget, was new to the series. He certainly made his mark! What an incredible choreographer.

Another highlight was Matt Baker when he did his *Austin Powers* jive. He got right into the character and really pulled it off. I know he's a former gymnast, but it's still impressive when you see a back somersault off the judges' desk – definitely a *Strictly* first.

Even after eight series, I love it more and more each time but for me last season raised the bar yet again. This year we have to go even bigger. Heaven help the cast of series nine. They've got an awful lot to live up to!

THE STORY OF SERIES 8

Lucky 8 Ball

It may have been the eighth series but there were plenty of firsts in *Strictly Come Dancing*'s class of 2010. To kick off the series the fourteen contestants were matched up with their dancing partners live on a red carpet launch show. Among them were the series' first psychologist, Pamela Stephenson, and first politician in the formidable form of Ann Widdecombe.

From Russia With Love

The professionals welcomed three new male dancers onto the floor. Jared Murillo, American star of *High School Musical*, England champ Robin Windsor and Russian Latin supremo Artem Chigvintsev. Soap star Kara Tointon was delighted when new partner Artem slid across the floor to her and later declared he came, 'from Russia with love'. Little did she know!

Setting the Scene

A sparkling new set was unveiled, complete with back screens and floors, which could be used to project images as the contestants danced, and a swanky new area for Tess, up above the dance floor. The delighted presenter said, 'It has a bird's eye view of all the dancing action going on behind us. I'm loving this. It's so posh.'

New Beginnings

The stars had been rehearsing for a group dance but were still in the dark about their partners. Singer Michelle Williams raised a cheer with a feisty, 'Bring them to mama!' before landing Brendan Cole, Natalie Lowe was beaming after nabbing soap hunk Scott Maslen and Paul Daniels, paired with Ola Jordan, declared, 'It's not even Christmas and I've pulled a cracker.'

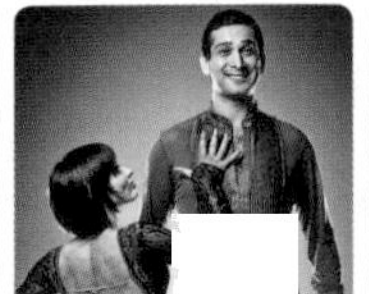

Acrobat Matt

Former gymnast Matt Baker upped the ante with an energetic cha cha cha starting with a front flip and cartwheel, which had Craig declaring, 'You, sir, are one to watch!'. Feisty granny Pamela admitted husband Billy Connolly might be jealous because *Strictly* is 'a licence to flirt outrageously.' She and James Jordan delivered a dreamy waltz which Alesha called 'breath-taking' and finished joint top, with Matt and Aliona, with 31.

Strictly The Good Life

Viewers got a double helping of *Strictly* as the competition kicked off with live shows on both Friday and Saturday. 'There's more tension in this room than there was in my nan's knicker elastic,' announced Len as the series began with a cha cha cha from *The Good Life* star Felicity Kendal and Vincent Simone, earning them a respectable 23.

From Magic To Tragic

Ola believed she had a few tricks up her sleeve that could turn TV magician Paul Daniels into a dancer but even making his partner appear in a trunk at the opening of his cha cha cha, didn't impress Craig, who said, 'The best part of that routine was the empty box.' Paul finished bottom of the table but, with no eviction in week 1, lived on to dance again.

Kara's Stumbling Start

In show 2 *EastEnder* Kara Tointon came out for her cha cha cha with all guns blazing but missed her footing. 'I was excited and I kept saying, as long as I don't fall over, I'll be so chuffed,' she said later. 'And as it happened I thought "oh no, it's live on television."' The judges forgave her and awarded the highest score of the night, with 30.

Soap Hunk Sexes It Up

EastEnder Scott Maslen was determined not to mess up on his first show. 'I messed up in the live *EastEnders* episode, I know better than most that you don't get a second chance.' Luckily he pulled of a surprisingly sexy waltz, which Len dubbed 'a tad raunchy' and Craig called 'dangerously romantic,' scoring 29.

Bruno's Meaner to Tina

Coronation Street star Tina O'Brien found the move from the Weatherfield cobbles to the dance floor nerve-racking, and fluffed up the steps in the cha cha cha. Bruno compared her to a 'baby doll Lolita, but she was upset when he told her, 'You went wrong so many times. If you go wrong, carry on.'

Nurse Patsy Raises the Pulse

After a nervous start in week 1, screen siren Patsy Kensit was determined to spice up the salsa for week 2 but filming her final scenes on *Holby* meant she and Robin had only four hours' training. Thrusting herself at the judges' table during the dance seemed to do the trick, with Bruno describing her as 'the killer jezebel with the pout.'

Dance Disappointment

Jimi Mistry's cha cha cha with Flavia also failed to impress the judges, with Craig comparing it to 'watching the scarecrow from the *Wizard of Oz*.' And Destiny's Child star Michelle Williams didn't prove too Bootylicious for head judge Len during her Latin number. 'Long legs, short skirt, bad technique,' he commented. And Craig added, 'Very stiff of hip. I was really disappointed.'

Gavin Gets the Guns Out

Rugby player Gavin Henson was also resorting to using his body, with a salsa routine that saw his shirt being ripped off. But his shyness was worrying the fearsome foursome. 'I can't believe someone as good-looking as you could look so self-conscious,' said Bruno. 'The six pack is not enough.' The fly-half's footwork earned him just 19 points.

Ann's Dance Debut

Asked what he was looking forward to on the launch show, Craig joked, 'Two words. Ann Widdecombe' and he wasn't alone. The former cabinet minister got a rousing reception for her waltz with Anton Du Beke, and greeted the judges' criticism with her usual aplomb. 'If you think that's bad, you should see the salsa,' she said. She scored one more than Paul, with 17.

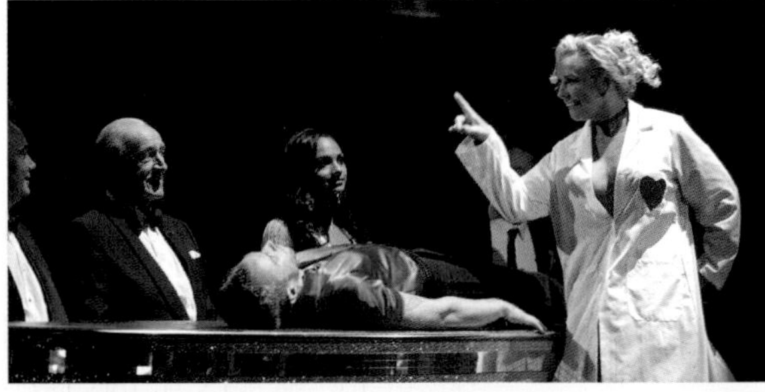

Doctor Beat

Psychologist Pamela Stephenson put partner James Jordan on the couch – or the judges' table – before ripping off her white coat and delivering a sizzling salsa. A stumble after a floor spin left her joking, 'I told him. James, you shouldn't throw granny on the floor.'

but Alesha declared her 'a force to be reckoned with.' With 32 points and a total of 63, she nailed the top spot on the leader board.

Going For Goldie

After a mauling from the panel for last week's cha cha cha, Goldie was determined to make an impression. But his 'smokin" foxtrot tribute to *The Mask* caused a judges' row after Bruno said he looked like he was 'slipping on a banana skin' and Craig said he was 'fantastic.' Despite a combined score of 46, the former Bond villain was in the last two with Peter Shilton and got his marching orders.

Tina Gets Scarlett's Fever

After nursing daughter Scarlett through a bout of chicken pox, soap star Tina was struck down herself and forced to pull out of the show in week 3. With Jared's family over from the states to watch, Tina was devastated, 'I feel like I'm letting everyone down,' she said from home. 'I feel really bad.' Jimi injured a tendon in his foot, but soldiered through to perform his rumba.

Great Scott

Despite declaring 'the fear is back', Scott managed a fabulous quickstep and proved he was King of the Swingers. An overwhelmed Bruno came up with the flirty catchphrase of the series, dubbing him 'Sssssscott!' But, with a score of 34, he was pipped to the post once again by Pamela, whose rumba got 35 and the first 'fab-u-lous!' of the series from Craig.

Quicksteps and Quick Tempers

Tempers bubbled over in training when Matt struggled with the quickstep and fiery redhead Aliona stormed out to cool off. The dance caused a rift between judges on the night, with Alesha claiming Matt was struggling to keep up while Bruno said 'You never lost timing' and Craig stated, 'I can't agree with Alesha that you had timing issues.'

Paul Conjures Up an Exit

Len was so impressed with Peter Shilton's quickstep he told him, 'if you're in the bottom two, I'll show me bum in Tesco's.' Luckily for the supermarket shoppers of Kent, he escaped. Instead Paul's rumba, which Craig dubbed 'infantile', guaranteed him a bottom slot and he was joined by Michelle. After the public vote, Paul did his disappearing act.

Kicks and Kisses

Week 4 and after a pelting from the judges in the previous week, Jimi Mistry put on an energetic show with his Charleston, praised by Len as 'great entertainment.' Tina reclaimed her place on the dance floor with the same dance, which Alesha called 'Springy, cheeky and quirky.' And Vincent ended his rumba with Felicity Kendal with a full on smacker, leaving them both smeared in lipstick.

Super-Ann

Politicians don't always keep their promises, but after vowing her week 4 tango had 'something so spectacular even I'm surprised', Ann certainly delivered. She brought the house down (not literally, of course) by flying down to the dance floor in a harness. Craig commented, 'It was gorgeous, ethereal, it was light, beautiful - and then you landed on the floor and that's when the problems began.'

Circus Tricks

Matt took Aliona back to stay on his own farm where they practised some dangerous lifts in a hay barn. On the night, Matt turned ringmaster with a handlebar moustache and astounded the audience by riding on to the dance floor on a unicycle. His Charleston was a triumph, with Bruno calling it, 'Showmanship in the tradition of the great Barnum.'

Peter Drops the Ballroom

With the mums on the school run greeting Scott Maslen with Bruno's saucy pronunciation of 'Sssssscott!' son Zack said 'I could hardly breathe it was SO embarrassing.' But Scott's hot tango earned him 35 and joint top place with Matt. At the bottom end, despite a morale boosting visit from Gary Lineker, goalkeeper Peter Shilton's Charleston scored 17 and earned him the red card.

Hallowe'en Horrors

In week 5, James Jordan went 'Extra mean for Hallowe'en' and put Pamela through hell in training, telling her, 'I'm not here to have fun, Pamela' and 'You've got a big bum so use it!' But the devilish duo failed to set the floor on fire during their jive, messed up a few steps and ended up with their lowest score of 27.

Tears and Tens

Emotions were running high in the Kara and Artem camp. The Russian accused her of being miserable before walking out and leaving her in tears. Kara confessed 'We're like a fiery married couple. I'm not enjoying this week at all.' But their *Phantom of the Opera* tango was a Hallowe'en hit, with Bruno calling it, 'Luscious drama, oozing with passion.' And it scored the first ten of the series, from Alesha.

Warps and All

After being called away the previous week due to a family bereavement, leaving Michelle in the capable hands of Ian Waite, Brendan was back and in fighting spirit. But the singer sprained her ankle in rehearsal for the jive and Hallowe'en brought out the worst in her partner, who argued with Len's verdict that the dance was more 'Time Warp' than jive. 'What you want to do, Brendan, is turn up, keep up and shut up!' said Len.

Gavin Unwrapped

Katya created a monster when she told Gavin to get aggressive in the paso doble. The Welsh dragon moaned, 'She wanted me to get into character. Now she's taking it personal.' When it came to the dance, Gav played the bare-chested matador and then ripped off Katya's demure dress to reveal a saucy red outfit. 'I love when you're coming out of your shell!' said Bruno. 'You have to reveal more of yourself.'

Snotty Scotty

The *EastEnders* hunk wasn't feeling too hot when he caught man flu. 'The Viennese waltz has a lot of spinning,' he said. 'And I have a lot of mucus, so that front row might expect a bit of slime. It's a Hallowe'en slimefest!' He battled through to perform a dance that Len called 'absolutely spellbinding' and landed three tens and a total of 39.

Tina Tangos Out

Anton literally swept the floor with Ann during the paso doble, which left Bruno declaring, 'I don't think I will ever recover from that ending!' They were bottom of the table with just 16. Tina struggled with the sultry side of the Argentine

tango and said, 'I just hope I don't scare the judges.' But Len called it, 'Your best dance to date.' The public chose to differ and the actress took her last bow.

Craig is Framed

In week 6 Ann and Anton upped the comedy ante with a hilarious Charleston and clever use of a prop. Beginning the dance gazing at a framed picture, Ann finished by revealing a portrait of nemesis Craig Revel Horwood. Alesha pointed out, 'It was more of a comedy sketch than a dance routine', and Craig joked that the thought of her kissing his picture was 'repulsive.'

Felicity is a Drag

Finding herself in the bottom two in week 5, Felicity had mixed emotions at Tina's departure. 'I was amazed at how emotional I was,' she said. 'She is a much better dancer than I am.' Vincent went topless during the paso doble, then dragged his partner across the floor to the judges' table – even after the music had ended. In response, Bruno called him, 'Gavin Henson – the pocket version.'

Crossing the Jordan
James was furious at the previous bad score and Pamela was bearing the brunt in training. Constantly reminding her of their low marks, he blew his top and stormed out. 'I'm not asking you for my health. I can dance!' But the foxtrot put them back on track with a score of 33 and Len assessing that 'the whole thing was beautiful.'

Hero to Zero
After scoring three tens in the previous week, Scott lost the plot with his rumba. Biggest fan Bruno told him, 'Sssscott! This week not quite so hot' and Alesha called it 'stagnant'. Craig said it 'jolted and jarred' and gave him just four points. Hot Scott found himself at the bottom end of the leader board, only just above Ann, for the first time.

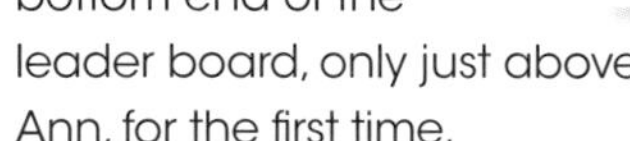

Matt Flack
Matt found himself in the centre of two rows yet again. First Aliona lost patience with him in training in what he politely called 'a little tiff', then Len lost his rag at Craig over the mention of a few missed heel leads. 'Not many,' shouted Len. 'Don't get pedantic! No, no.' Craig went on to attack Matt's thumbs – so not picky at all! He scored 35 but missed out to Kara's scorching salsa by one point.

Jimi's Mistry Departure
East is East star Jimi was convinced nine-year-old daughter Ellie was 'very proud of her dancing dad.' But when he visited her school, she hid her face and protested, 'It was really embarrassing!' His quickstep caused another judges' row as Craig called it 'heavy' and an outraged Bruno insisted 'Are you kidding! He was walking on air.' Jimi was chuffed with his highest score of 32. Sadly it wasn't enough to save him from the public vote.

Patsy Blossoms
Week 7 and Patsy Kensit showed she was no longer an *Absolute Beginner*. Smarting from a 'cha cha cha chavvy' remark from Craig, she set about making herself into a lady for the Viennese waltz, and Robin balanced books on her head to help her posture. This time the acerbic Aussie called her 'Classy, confident' and she matched Pamela's 32.

Pam's Highland Fling
Pamela treated James to a break at the palatial Aberdeen home she shares with Billy. The pair met local schoolchildren, chatted to a few cows and James even tossed a caber. And she introduced him to a new style of dance, at the village ceilidh. The fresh Scottish air did him good and their cha cha cha won them 32 points and James' first ever trip to Blackpool.

Bruno Gets Gav-Love

Rugby tough guy Gavin came over all soppy when he saw his kids on the video before taking the floor. 'I now only see them two or three times a week and it is hard,' he admitted. 'It got to me when I saw them on the VT.' But it didn't stop him snogging Bruno at the start of the quickstep, leaving the Italian judge breathless, and grabbing a high score of 33.

Scott's Back in Business

Bruno's aftershave was working wonders as Natalie became the second celeb to plant a smacker on him. And after last week's defeat, Scott came back fighting with their jumping jive to 'Hit the Road Jack' which Craig called 'Finger-licking good!' While he kicked and flicked his way to three tens, beating Kara's two for the Argentine tango, the audience booed Craig for awarding a nine!

Granny in a Tangle

Ann sailed through on the public vote once again and Felicity got a boost when her grandchildren popped in during salsa training and formed their own judges' panel. But Vincent's complicated armography, with the actress turning while still holding his hands, proved a sticking point. Bruno said, 'You got yourself into a bit of a tangle' and Craig called in 'a minor disaaaaster'. With 26 they were in the bottom two with Michelle but scraped through.

Visa Runs Out For Michelle

Paso doble needs plenty of aggression and most of it was in the training room for Michelle and Brendan. He claimed 'I am really being patient today', before yelling at his partner. Michelle lost her rag and stormed out shouting, 'be quiet and let me get it!' After the dance, she told the judges, 'whatever you are about to say I agree.' Craig called it, 'gnarled, knotty, nodulistic' and the Destiny's Child singer's fate was sealed.

Blackpool Bound

The eight remaining celebs headed north for week 8 to the famous Tower Ballroom and Patsy was determined to put on a show. After some lessons from scantily dressed samba dancers she was ready to get the party started but she missed her footing on the night. Bruno thought she was, 'glitzy and sexy. Like a true Vegas scrumpet!' But her score of 28 left her battling in the elimination zone.

Artem's a Smooth Operator

Kara was devastated when an awkward lift in American smooth training left Artem with a damaged shoulder hours before the show. The tearful actress

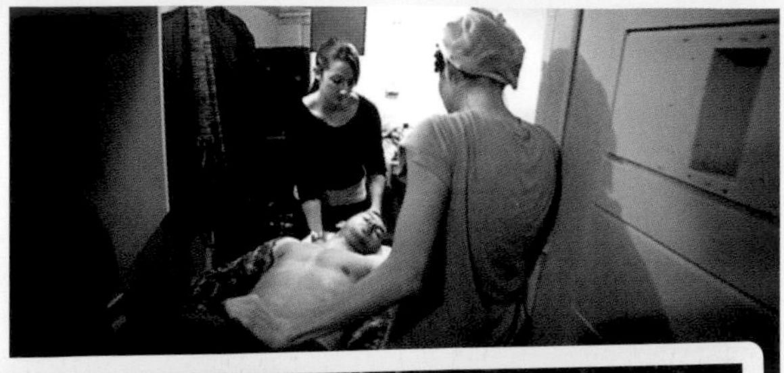

said, 'I felt my whole bodyweight crush his head.' But the Russian battled through with a stunning smooth which Alesha called, 'Seductive, smooth, intense.' Despite two tens, the pair were slammed by Len for the lack of hold. He awarded them a 6, and Blackpool responded with a chorus of boos.

Gymnastic Matt

Despite consistently high scores Matt was still chasing the perfect ten. 'I really want to go out there and nail it,' he said. His lively samba ended with a triple backflip, which impressed the audience and three of the judges. But Len wasn't 'too keen on them flip-flops at the end.' Even so, Matt bagged his first two tens and a total score of 38.

Gavin Gets Emotional

Divorced dad Gavin admitted he messed up his previous dance because he saw his kids on the VT and 'had a moment'. He added, 'there's only one thing that makes me emotional and that's my kids.' With difficult lifts in the American smooth this week, he was keen 'to prove my muscles aren't just for show.' But nerves got the better of him again, he missed some steps and Craig called the dance 'lame and lacklustre'.

Smooth Exit

After two weeks in the bottom two, Vincent was beginning to despair 'Where are my women?' he asked. 'They should be voting for me. Where are they? Doing the dishes?' But the smooth Italian and partner Felicity failed to win the public over with their American smooth. Despite their highest score of 30, *The Good Life* star was knocked out.

A Comedy Turn

Alesha crowned Pamela 'Queen of Blackpool' after her American smooth, which Craig called 'Gorgeous' and which earned her first two tens. At the other end of the scale Ann and Anton entertained the crowd in a spirited samba with the usual elements, such as the samba rolls, vetoed by Ann as 'improper'. Craig said it was 'overwhelmingly awful' and they scored the lowest samba mark ever, with 13.

Jive Talking

In week 9, Artem received a ribbing over his shoulder injury from Anton, who said, 'How about we swap? Then you can get a bad shoulder, a bad back, your hips'll go, the knees will start to creak...' This week Artem added tonsillitis to his list of woes, leaving

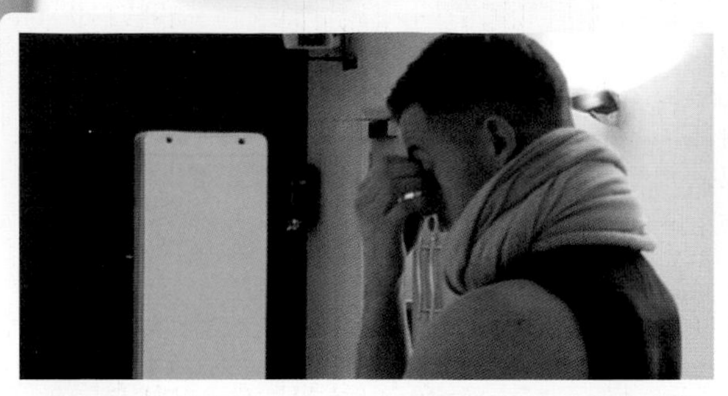

him feeling 'cursed'. Their jive was so impressive that Len joked, 'It steamed up my glasses,' but Craig only awarded a seven over timing issues and they finished with 34.

Titanic Sinks
Ann and Anton went overboard in their rumba, with a tribute to the smash hit movie *Titanic*, complete with iceberg. As Ann stood on the bow of the ship, Anton emerged from the fog on the floor in what Len called, 'the daftest dance I have ever seen'. Craig called it 'a testament to bad dancing,' and awarded them a 1, giving them 14.

Sleepy Scott
Mixing training with his work on *EastEnders* was taking its toll on Scott. Having had two days off in nine weeks he was literally falling asleep on the job and his American smooth proved a little bumpy. Craig called it 'a terrible shame' and 'a complete disaaaaaster', and Len advised, 'try and stay awake and come back stronger.' He still bagged 31 points, despite an unpopular six from Craig.

Nice Try, Gav
As Katya tried to release Gavin's true feelings in training he let rip with 'I hate the jive!'. On the night the rugby star tried to win over the judges by shaking his booty in their faces, prompting Craig's comment, 'That bottom wiggle was unnecessary and it smacks of desperation.' But Alesha thought he was 'cute' and added, 'I just wanted to give you a big hug.'

Pamela Misbehaves
The charleston had Pamela holding James off the floor in a cartwheel, a move which the psychologist said left him with 'trust issues' in training. 'Pamela is 61 next week,' he argued ungallantly. 'No wonder I'm worried.' Watched by Pam's two daughters, however, the school-themed dance, to 'Let's Misbehave', was a triumph. 'It tickled my fancy,' said Len, and they were top of the class with 38.

Len Plays the Villain
After being booed in Blackpool, Len was cast in the bad guy role again and this time he had a sidekick. Alesha upset the audience when she said she was 'disappointed' by Matt's American smooth. Len got the same reaction when he told the presenter, 'Normally you're really good, tonight you're nearly good.' Matt still scored a respectable 33.

Patsy's Painful Parting

Holby actress Patsy was in need of a doctor when her toe swelled up after weeks of repetitive dance moves. 'Luckily the routine this week has a chair in it,' she joked. 'I'm hoping to have a nice little sit for 16 bars.' While she made it through, Bruno complained her Argentine tango lacked, 'that fleshy, carnal, passionate feel.' Patsy scored 30 but she became a casualty of the public vote.

Matt Finds his Mojo

A tribute to *Austin Powers* saw Matt and Aliona getting groovy in the jive but training proved a chilly affair as the *CountryFile* frontman was filming in the snow-covered Outer Hebrides. With airports closed the pair only just made it back in time and Matt started the dance with a flip off the judges' desk. 'Groovy baby!' said Bruno. 'I could have been in Carnaby Street in 1965.' The couple matched Scott's score of 35.

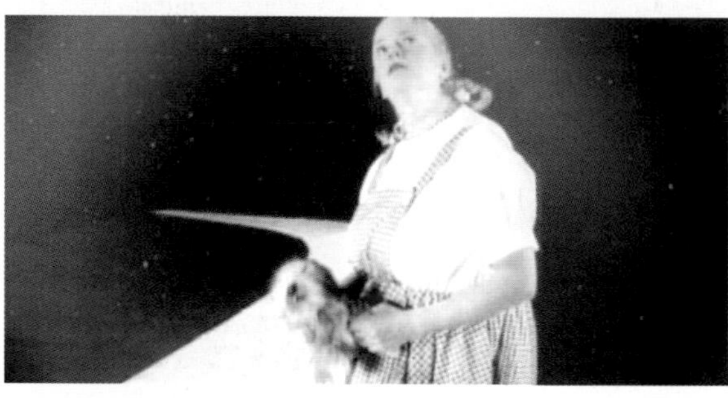

Strictly Goes to Hollywood

The quarter-finals brought a touch of Tinseltown glamour to the *Strictly* studio with a movie special. The remaining celebs opened the show in a *Star Wars* spoof, which ended with 'one woman set on intergalactic dance domination' – Ann dressed as Dorothy from *Wizard of Oz*. The professionals performed tributes to *Grease*, *Top Gun*, *Pulp Fiction* and *Easter Parade* and the couples embarked on a night of movie magic.

Pamela's Birthday Treat

Former funnygirl Pamela celebrated her 61st birthday with James and joked, 'You're only as old as the man you feel so I'm currently about 32.' After cake and champagne it was back to work on the *Ghost*-themed Viennese waltz, which the judges thought was out of this world. Craig said it was 'Graceful, elegant, stylish, tasteful, full of emotion – gorgeous!' The perfect score of 40 was the best birthday present of the day.

Licence to Thrill

Scott fulfilled a boyhood dream by becoming James Bond for his paso doble, with Natalie as his sexy Bond girl in an Ursula Andress-style bikini. She insisted he got his chest out for the routine, and he despaired, 'I'm forty. I've got a hairy chest. Gavin's on the show, dammit!' But Craig called it 'virile, red hot' and Len dubbed him 'Double 0 se-VEN!'

Gavin Gets the Blues

The Welsh dragon was breathing fire after the mauling from the judges' for the previous week's dance, but for their *Blues Brothers* routine he vowed that he and Katya were 'on a mission.' Their foxtrot to 'Minnie the Moocher' gained them a standing ovation and had Alesha calling them 'a sexy, hot couple.' They gained 11 points on the previous week, with 33. Mission accomplished.

Love on the Dance Floor

Kara's movie homage was the famous 'Roxanne' tango from *Moulin Rouge* and it seems the passion was spilling over into the rehearsal room. Artem admitted his feelings on camera but vowed to wait. 'It's going to happen after *Strictly* is over,' he said. 'I'm confirming the rumours.' On the night, Alesha declared their 38-point tango, 'mesmerising' and Bruno, 'spectacular'.

Hello Dolly, Goodbye Widdy

Anton admitted 'our American may not be quite so smooth,' and the judges thought Ann's dancing was finally getting beyond a joke. 'For me the honeymoon is over' said Alesha, after the *Hello Dolly* routine. With the dance's lowest score ever, she had broken five *Strictly* records and spent eight weeks at the bottom of the leader board but the former MP had finally lost her seat.

Getting in the Swing

For the semi-finals, the five remaining couples had to learn two new dances as well as take part in a *Strictly* swingathon, where they would dance together until they were tapped on the shoulder and asked to leave the floor. 'We want to see lifts, tricks, high energy and everything that can make the king of swing – or maybe the queen,' said Len. 'This is truly the war on the floor.'

Judges go Gaga for Pamela

'Learning one dance in a week is very tough,' said Pamela in rehearsals. 'Learning three is ridiculous.' But her paso doble to 'Bad Romance' had Bruno doing his best Lady Gaga impression with a 'Pamela-ah-ah, ah-ah-Ooh-la-la,' scoring 35. And her quickstep was declared 'Fab-U-lous!' by Craig, earning her the second perfect score of the series.

Liftgate

Kara and Artem's Viennese waltz caused a judges' row when Craig thought her foot had come off the floor in an illegal lift. Alesha and Bruno protested and Len said, 'Don't listen to fanlight fanny at the end.' With Craig dropping a point they scored 39,

and history repeated itself after their stunning rumba when he told her, 'If you hadn't put that lift in, darling, I might have dusted off my ten.' Another 39, plus a win in the swingathon, put them top of the table.

Matt Falls Flat

For the salsa, Matt swapped places with Aliona, who opened the dance on the judges' desk. Sadly, she gained no extra sway with the fearsome foursome who ripped into the routine with Len saying he was 'disappointed' and Craig calling it 'insipid'. The couple bounced back with a triumphant tango, which Bruno called 'Strong, powerful, driven.' Two tens gave a score of 38.

Gav's Kicked into Touch

Before the semis Gavin lamented, 'I think we're all aware that there's been a top four – Pamela, Kara, Matt and Scott – and I'm on the outside of that.' He was first out of the swingathon and scored 27 points for his samba, which Craig said 'lacked rhythm'. But after a passable Viennese waltz, Len called him 'my hero' for coming back fighting every time and Alesha said 'you are the most improved.' Sadly he was first to go in the double elimination.

Scott to Trot Off

Scott's Argentine tango failed to impress three judges and Bruno was the only one who picked up the 'film noir' nuance in the routine. 'Is it a lover or a stalker?' he said. 'You never gave it away.' His nautically themed Charleston also tickled the Italian judge who said, 'after seven months at sea you'd found a flapper and you're ready for action!' But the second eviction saw the sailor walk the plank.

Tears and Triumph

After 11 weeks jostling for the top of the table, Pamela, Kara and Matt were worthy opponents for the Grand Final. And emotions were running high. Matt welled up as he recalled getting through, saying, 'It's such a special feeling to know that you're there.' Kara wept as she talked about Artem. 'He is so special,' she blubbed. 'And I think lifting the glitterball with him would be amazing.' Even tough teacher James Jordan shed a tear as he got through to his first-ever final. 'I didn't realise James was so overemotional,' marvelled Pamela. 'He's actually enormously sensitive.'

Pamela Bows Out

'I bet James took one look at me and thought, "dumpy psychologist, I'll give it two weeks",' joked Pamela at the final. But he couldn't have been prouder when she repeated the perfect score for

the Viennese waltz, which Bruno described as 'Simply brilliant.' The couple's showdance to *Dirty Dancing*'s 'Time of my Life' also won high praise, with Len calling it 'Charming' and Craig, 'Fantastic.' Pam was top of the judges' table with 77 out off 80 and James quipped, 'Nobody puts granny in the corner!' Sadly, with their scores just a guide, it was all down to viewers' votes and the sexy senior was forced to sit out.

The Final Showdown

Former *Blue Peter* presenter Matt chose a samba he'd made earlier as his first dance, matching the 38 he got in Blackpool. For his showdance, he went back to his gymnastic training with a routine that included cartwheels, backward and forward rolls, breakdancing rolls and flips, and a handless cartwheel from a huge box. Len said, 'A few too many stunts and tricks for me,' but he scored 34. His paso doble had Craig cast as the good guy, praising his 'port de bras' and saying, 'I actually rather liked it,' as the other three judges slammed his technique and his final Viennese waltz had Len praising, 'you're an excellent dancer, and an excellent ballroom dancer.' In total Matt picked up 144 out of a possible 160 points.

Glitterball Glory

Kara and Artem's dances caused controversy amongst the judges. Their near perfect rumba was once more penalised by Craig for a lift while her American smooth had steam coming out of Len's ears for 'a whole dance out of hold, which is supposed to be 40 per cent in hold.' After injuring her arm doing a backflip in the showdance, Kara battled through two more dances and the couple ended up with a score of 150 out of 160. On winning the show the tearful twosome, whose last dance had been to the classic track 'Cry Me a River', dissolved in floods once again as Kara gushed, 'This has been the most special experience of my life.'

Queen Kara

To the viewing nation, Kara Tointon's final dances were poetry in motion. But the *Strictly* champ still can't bring herself to watch the waltz and the American smooth, because she reckons she danced like a robot!

'I looked awful. I hurt my arm in the second dance, the showdance, and I nearly had to pull out,' she explains. 'I was given some cocodamol because I couldn't actually move my arm and I remember thinking, "Oh my God, I'm going to have to drop out." I was steeling myself to tell them I couldn't do the last two dances even if we got through. Then the co-codamol kicked in and I was in a bit of a daze. I don't remember any of it. But when I watched it back I could see that I'm not really with it. I danced like a robot. I can't watch it because I get really upset.'

Thankfully, the public didn't agree and the famous glitterball trophy was hers. For the former *EastEnders* star it marked the end of a rollercoaster ride which began with her worst nightmare – a cha cha cha disaster in week 1.

'The first week I loved the dance but I was wearing something quite outrageous and I was not confident enough at that point,' she recalls. 'It was something that professionals would wear, and I guess it was a bit too much. Then I tripped over the skirt and I went down. It was my worst nightmare, to fall over, and it happened in the first week. So after a few tears I realised that the worst had happened now and my biggest fear, falling over, had come true. So the only way was up.'

Even though she hit the deck, Kara also hit the high marks, starting her *Strictly* experience with 30 and firmly planting herself in the top four slots she was to share throughout the series with Scott Maslen, Matt Baker and Pamela Stephenson. The following weeks brought tears and triumphs, hard work and hard knocks, high drama and high marks. And to add a little spice into the mix, Kara and her dancing partner Artem Chigvintsev, began to fall in love.

'I wasn't expecting that,' says the ever-candid Kara. 'Going into it I said, I was determined I wouldn't end up with my dance partner. I even did a press conference and said, "I'm not having a relationship for at least two years," and I meant it. But a couple of weeks in, I thought, "Oh no! Here we go. He's gorgeous and he's lovely as well." It was the last thing I wanted to happen but that's life – when you're not planning for something to happen, that's when things fall in your lap.'

Initially, the pair were wary of their feelings and vowed to put their burgeoning romance on hold until after the series. Being in an artificially intense experience, they reasoned, it would be hard to keep their feelings in perspective.

'I was so worried about making anything of it because it was a weird situation,' she says. 'You're together every day in a strange environment, you're being filmed and obviously I knew there was something there but we both thought, "Is this a holiday romance? When the show comes to an end, would we find that what was there was only there because of the circumstances?" You can't answer those questions until the show is over. I knew I'd found someone very special but it wasn't until after the final that we were able to really get to know each other, outside of the

Strictly environment and to do normal things that couples do. I'm chuffed that it turned out as I'd hoped, but I didn't know that it would at the time.'

Despite emerging triumphant at the end of the series, Kara admits she was very apprehensive going into the show and reveals she had been due to take part in the previous series, but got cold feet.

'If you are an actor or actress people never really see you as you, so throwing myself into something where I have to be myself on screen made me really nervous,' she says. 'I'd only just left *EastEnders* and I woke up in a hot sweat and thought "I can't do it this year" because I really wanted to give acting a go. I'm glad I had that year because when series eight came round and I hadn't done any acting at all, I knew that if they asked me again I would jump at the opportunity.

'*Strictly* is massive, it takes over your life, more than I imagined, for four months, and I knew I'd love the experience but I was so apprehensive. I had all the wrong ideas because I was so worried and actually it was great just to let go, forget about everything else in your life and just concentrate on learning this amazing new skill.'

Stumble aside, Kara showed potential from day one and the judges' comments got more admiring with each stunning routine. In week 5, Bruno declared her Hallowe'en paso doble, 'Luscious drama, oozing with passion,' and Alesha awarded it the first ten of the series. For Kara, it was a turning point.

'My favourite moment was performing the paso doble because it suddenly all fell into place and I got my mojo,' she reveals. 'And I realised that week that actually the audience want you to enjoy it and to do your best, so there's no need to be nervous. I guess that was the moment I let all my inhibitions go.'

In week 8, disaster struck when Artem suffered an injured shoulder in rehearsals for the American smooth, and their Blackpool performance looked touch and go for a while. Even so, it remains her favourite dance.

'That dance was really special because Blackpool was so amazing as a building, and to dance there was wonderful,' she says. 'I didn't realise until I got there how special that would be.'

The following week, due to the injury and a bout of tonsillitis, Artem was laid low for a few days. The result

My favourite moment was performing the paso doble because it suddenly all fell into place and I got my mojo

was a less-than-spectacular jive which Kara counts as her worst moment on the show.

'It's so nerve-racking on a Saturday and there's nothing worse than going out there and not knowing your dance,' she admits. 'That happened to me in jive week because we only had a few days to rehearse that week. I went out there that night and I wasn't able to enjoy it because I didn't really know what I was doing. I really wanted to do a good jive because I love the dance but it was rubbish. After that I thought, "Now I'm going to put everything in. I can't do that again."'

Looking back on her months in Strictly, Kara confesses she went into it with low expectations, hoping to survive for the first few weeks. And even her nearest and dearest didn't believe she could win it.

'My family said, "Just go and have a good time, there's no way you'll win something like this," and I didn't think I could, not in a million years,' she laughs. 'I knew I'd love the dancing and love the training, and I knew I wanted to stay in as long as possible but I didn't see the latter stages as something that would be likely. I thought I'd probably make it to week 4 or 5, if I'm lucky. But slowly, as the weeks go on, you start to love it more and you don't want to go home, so I tried harder and harder and I loved it, every week, even more.'

Since winning the show, Kara's feet have barely touched the ground. After the *Strictly Come Dancing* tour, in January and February, it was straight off to trek across the deserts of Africa for Comic Relief, where months of dancing provided her with a distinct advantage. 'Everyone else got blisters and awful problems but I think the dancing got me fit enough for it, and my feet had hardened up, so I didn't get any blisters,' she says. On her return she was straight into rehearsals for a starring role in the West End production of *Pygmalion*, opposite Rupert Everett.

As well as meeting Artem, and a whole host of new friends in the fellow celebrities and professionals, the stunning actress has noticed one more major change in her life since her *Strictly* win.

'When you're in something like *EastEnders* people don't see you as an actress, they see you as the character, and not a lot of people really liked the character of Dawn, because she was quite a bolshy person.

'*Strictly* has made people call me Kara, and I'd been answering to Dawn for so long I'd got used to that. I didn't answer to my name any more, so it was nice to have strangers finally calling me Kara!'

And she insists that her initial fears in taking the challenge were completely unfounded. 'All my worries now seem silly because it is a lovely entertainment show, it's not too serious, it's just a bit of fun, and to anyone who is thinking of doing it I would personally recommend it,' she says. 'You learn so much about yourself. It was a life-changing experience and it's given me so much. I've absolutely fallen in love with dancing – I love it.'

Alesha

Unleashes Her Verdict

Four years ago Alesha Dixon waltzed her way into the nation's hearts and lifted the glitterball trophy for herself. And in September 2009, she became a permanent fixture on the *Strictly* set, casting a critical eye over the competing celebrities as they chase those elusive 10s. For the former champ, watching the trials and tribulations of the hopeful hoofers brings memories of her own tears and triumphs flooding back.

'Winning *Strictly Come Dancing* changed my life but being a contestant is only to be done once,' she says. 'I now relive my experience through the other contestants. It reminds me of that special time and it's like an emotional rollercoaster all over again.'

As the only judge who has been through dance training herself, she has a particular empathy with the contestants. For that reason, perhaps, she has been the first to award a perfect score in the last two series – for Ricky Whittle's Viennese waltz and Kara Tointon's Argentine tango. But Alesha is happy to be the kindest member of the fearsome foursome, and believes the judges' job is to help contestants improve, not shoot them down in flames.

'I want to be myself and as honest as I can,' she says. 'I respect the show and what it is all about and I want to see the same from the contestants. It's important to be helpful and give people advice so they can work on things.'

As last season was her second stint on the panel, Alesha felt more settled and she admits that she enjoyed the shows more than ever.

'I have the best seat in the house and I feel completely at home as a judge,' she reveals. 'I also feel honoured to have been a part of what I believe is the best *Strictly* series yet.'

What made last year's *Strictly* so special?
I think the new set is fabulous. When I was a contestant I would've loved to have danced on it. It's so much bigger and better now. And I was so excited at the line-up. Such a diverse bunch. Like a pack of liquorice allsorts!

What was your favourite use of props?
I think Ann and Anton had the best use of a prop when they performed *Titanic*, with the ship's bell and iceberg, although I did also love Natalie and Scott's performance around the cauldron for the Hallowe'en special.

Who did you think were the best dancers?
My favourite dancers were Pamela, Patsy, Scott and of course the amazing Kara! They all did very well, with Pamela and Kara being the most consistent throughout. Matt Baker was also very strong from the beginning. They were extremely strong contestants considering some of them had never danced before. It's always so lovely to see people catch the *Strictly* bug and improve week on week.

'Your bum looks great in those trousers!'

What were the highlights of the series?
Ann was one of the highlights of every show! She was pure pantomime and I loved every minute of it. She gave as good as she got and I always thought 'fair play to her'. There were so many incredible moments but mainly Ann and Anton! Blackpool was exciting too and Kara lifting the trophy was very special.

Who surprised you the most?
I think Matt Baker was the biggest surprise. The first time he danced we were all impressed and felt he had great potential. I thought Michelle Williams would have been a stronger dancer but she seemed a bit fragile at times, and Felicity was exceptionally bendy. I never saw that coming.

Who improved the most?
To a certain extent they all improved. After the first few weeks the competition really gets going and they all raised their game. After a shaky start, I thought Patsy Kensit was a delight to watch because she was growing in confidence each week.

Did you miss the dance off?
Every now and then when you fear you may lose a great dancer you miss the dance off but I believe the public has the right to decide. They're spending their money to keep in their favourite so it should be their choice.

What were the best and worst dances?
The best dance of the series for me was Kara and Artem's *Moulin Rouge* tango in Hollywood week. Both of their tangoes were superb. They completely took my breath away. The worst dance was probably so boring I can't remember.

How dangerous is sitting next to Bruno?
I love sitting next to Bruno because he is so much fun! Full of energy and joy! He's flamboyant and extroverted and we love him for it. He is one of a kind, but I fear next time I may need a shield or helmet to protect myself from his unpredictable outbursts!

Are you excited about series 9?
The next series has a lot to live up to but it always gets better. I have no doubt about that. With new dancers and new personalities who knows what awaits us? And that's the beauty of *Strictly*, you'll just have to wait and see.

Alesha's Observations:

On Michelle and Brendan's Hallowe'en jive
'It's kind of how I would imagine Tina Turner would do the jive. You're both barking mad. Well done.'

On Matt's week 2 foxtrot
'I wasn't sure you could do sexy but you just proved me wrong. I think that's the sexiest foxtrot I've ever seen.'

On Pamela's week 2 salsa
'I love you Pamela. Your body moves effortlessly. That had everything I expect from a salsa. It was sexy, it had control throughout. Best of the night. You're a force to be reckoned with.'

After Gavin Henson's rumba in week 3
'Your bum looks great in those trousers!'

After Ann's week 6 Charleston
'The actress is emerging. I love the opening with the picture frame. For me it was more of a comedy sketch than a dance routine. The only sign of the Charleston was the headband but it was thoroughly enjoyable.'

After Patsy's week 7 Viennese waltz
'You're an actress but there's nothing fake about the way you dance. You may not be the queen of technique but you dance with your heart.

On Ann's *Titanic* rumba in week 9
'Kate Winslet eat your heart out! My favourite storyline of the series and I could see genuine love between you.'

Alex Jones

One Show star Alex Jones was spurred on to take part in *Strictly* by co-presenter Matt Baker, whose acrobatic routines saw him grab second place in the last series. 'Matt really encouraged me and he kept saying how much of a great time he's had,' she says. 'Yes, it's hard work but it's been an absolutely unforgettable experience for him. And it helped to know that Matt would be a fantastic support during the process, so I've got somebody with me daily who understands how difficult it is and how fantastic it is as well.'

Even so, she admits her flexible friend is a hard act to follow. 'Matt is generally extremely gifted at everything he does. He was incredibly talented and he worked hard. I work hard but Matt's competiveness is second to none.'

While Matt was famous for his backflips and cartwheels Alex, who is paired with James Jordan, is sticking to the more conventional steps.

'On the first day of training James said, "So Matt brought backflips to the table. What do you bring?" and I said, "a backward roll!" I think that's the level of my gymnastics so you won't see many acrobatics in our routine. If you do, I'll be as surprised as you are.'

The 34-year-old presenter was born in Ammanford in Wales and studied Theatre, Film and TV at Aberystwyth University. After graduating she worked as a TV researcher before joining Welsh language TV channel S4C as a presenter on singing programme *Cân i Gymru* (*A Song for Wales*). In July 2010, she took over from former *Strictly* contestant Christine Bleakley on *The One Show* and has since become a household name.

Alex is hoping that the viewers who watch her discussing serious issues on a daily basis will see the fun side of her. 'On *The One Show* people get to know you up to a point and there's only so much of yourself you can show, because I sometimes have to be quite straight, so hopefully people will get to know what I'm really like. And I can show that I actually do have legs, because all we do is sit down!'

While she's prepared to work hard, she is keen to have a few laughs along the way. 'The only thing that's going to carry me through is humour,' she says. 'I'm pretty realistic, which I think is quite important. At the start, I was more awful than I expected. I can't believe how bad I actually was. But I'm seeing a little bit of progress every day. I'm not a professional dancer, I am a novice. It's going to take a long time and that's the best view you can have because otherwise you'll get upset with yourself and you're not going to enjoy the experience. It's bound to get tougher but I think instead of dreading what's to come, I want to enjoy it now and see how it goes.'

> When you hit the dance floor you have to take on a persona and the costumes are a big part of that. I say chuck as many sequins at me as you possibly can!

And she's looking forward to modelling the ballgowns and skimpy Latin outfits on the show. 'The frocks are lovely, although I've not been as naked as I was on the launch show, apart from in the shower! But you have to get 100 per cent into it. When you hit the floor you have to take on a persona and the costumes are a big part of that. I say, chuck as many sequins at me as you possibly can!'

Audley Harrison

Boxing legend Audley Harrison is following in the not-so-dainty footsteps of his fellow sportsmen, who have bobbed and weaved through both *Strictly* and *Dancing with the Stars* without knocking out the opposition. But he is hoping he can improve on the prancing pugilists' records.

'I am hoping to do better than boxers in the past,' he says. 'In America we've had Sugar Ray Leonard, Floyd Mayweather and Evander Holyfield and the UK have had Joe Calzaghe. I would never claim to be as good as Joe Calzaghe in the ring, but I definitely think I've got him whooped on the dance floor!'

Londoner Audley was already at college when he discovered his talent. After a fight with another student, he was asked if he was a boxer and invited to try out at a ring. In 1997, he became British Super Heavyweight Champion. A year later he retained the title and picked up a Gold medal at the 1998 Commonwealth Games and in 2000, he won Gold at the Sydney Olympics by defeating Mukhtarkhan Dildabekov of Kazakhstan and was also awarded an MBE.

In 2004, Harrison relocated to the USA where he was unbeaten in 11 fights, with eight knockouts. But living stateside has caused a headache for training with his British-based training partner Natalie Lowe.

'My daughter Ariella has just started school and my wife Raychel was in the middle of starting a business, so it could only work if I was going to be home in September. Natalie choreographed the dance and then *Strictly* found me two dancers who worked on the American show to fill the gap. It hasn't been plain sailing, but that's always the case for Audley Harrison – nothing's ever easy.'

Audley arrived back in the UK a week before the start of the show, so he could put the routine together with Natalie, and Raychel and five-year-old Ariella were on hand to watch his first dance. 'They're keen to see me dance, so they came over for the first show and then my daughter's had to go back to school. Daddy's showing a different side so it's going to be fun.'

I've got to recognise I'm 39 and I have injuries but that's not going to stop me dancing and enjoying myself

The boxing legend is still as competitive as ever but says past injuries means he will have to be sensible. 'I'm the bionic man,' he laughs. 'No athlete is ever injury free. I've had more operations than the average person so there's always that risk. I do intend to go back to boxing. Ten years ago I wanted to win at all cost, but now I'm older and wiser and I can't go all out. I've got to recognise I'm 39 and I have injuries, but that's not going to stop me dancing and enjoying myself.'

After twenty years in the ring, Audley has some serious muscle lurking under his tight Latin shirts. But if the female fans want to see him get the guns out, they'll have to put their voting fingers to work.

'I haven't been boxing since last year so I will not be taking off my shirt for the first few weeks,' he teases. 'If the ladies want to see my six-pack, they'll have to keep me in the competition!'

Matt Baker may have gone away empty-handed on the night of the series 8 final but his antics and acrobatics entertained the nation until the bitter end. From the opening sequence of his week one cha cha cha, when he performed a flip and a cartwheel, The *Country File* host had us hooked. Despite his background as a British gymnastics champ, however, he admits it had been a long time since he'd indulged in such spectacular stunts.

'I'd packed it in when I was 16, and I was 32 when I did *Strictly*,' he says. 'Lots of people do sport when they're young and not so much when they're older. What I got from the gymnastics was the dedication and the ability to apply myself to a cause. I focused in, I went for it and I thrived in it as well, I really did. I loved getting back into that mind-set and training hard. Gymnastics also helps a little bit as far as co-ordination but I did start doing tricks that I was doing when I was 16 and it was still scary doing them live on television.'

Acrobat Matt continued to show off his skills in every possible routine, often to the irritation of head judge and dance purist Len Goodman. After a triple backflip at the end of his high scoring samba, Len moaned, 'I wasn't keen on those flip-flops at the end.' When he told the other judges, 'They know I don't like it so they put it in just to annoy me,' Craig quipped, 'I would do 17 backflips just to annoy Len!'

One trick Len did approve of, however, was the back somersault off the judges' desk during the *Austin Powers* inspired jive. 'I liked the backflip thing,' he said. 'I thought this table was going to break so I was so relieved when you got off of it!' But Matt has let us in on a shocking secret behind the risky stunt.

'I didn't actually practise the back somersault I did in the jive, so that was the first time I'd done it,' he reveals. 'I knew, because of the way the stomach muscles work, if I did that in training I would rip my stomach muscles and I wouldn't be able to work or train for days. So I did that somersault, with Cuban heels on, in front of a live audience on Saturday night TV, having not practised it or done anything like that for 16 years! I had to have three days to recover afterwards because it did rip my stomach muscles. But you've got to push it out there if you want to be successful. You don't play safe.'

Matt vividly recalls being asked to take part in the show and admits he needed no persuasion. 'There was no doubt in my mind,' he laughs. 'I actually found out on my daughter Molly's birthday that I was going to be doing it. We were all in the car, travelling home from the London Aquarium, the phone call came and I said to my wife. "What do you reckon?" But it was a

One trick Len did approve of, however, was the back somersault off the judges' desk during the *Austin Powers* inspired jive.

no-brainer, we were so excited! I've wanted to do it for a long time and I was asked a while back when I was on *Blue Peter*, but it just wasn't possible. This time, the timing was right, I could fit it into my schedule and just went for it 100%.

'I was still on *Country File* so we had a good chat, with both teams, about whether or not it would work out logistically, and we decided that we could train while we're on location and that whoever my dance partner would be they would have to just come with me.'

As he was teamed with redhead Aliona Vilani, it meant he could give his teacher an education of her own. 'It was an experience for her because coming from Kazakhstan, she got to see Britain and travel all over the country,' he recalls. 'Everywhere we went we used the community centres and the school halls, and hotels would put the wedding disco floors out for us and we felt an enormous amount of support. It felt like we were doing it for everybody else, and all these people were behind us, and that was the beauty of what we got from our experience. A lot of people trained in the same place all the time but we didn't use the same place more than three or four times and every week we were somewhere different.'

With Matt's determination and drive, and Aliona's tough teaching methods, the pair made perfect partners.

'Aliona was a hard taskmaster, but I was a willing pupil so I was up for as much as she wanted to push me. She would have a focused idea about what she wanted to achieve in that week, and I would be just as ambitious and want to do what she asked. We would be pushing it right up to the last minute. We'd be out in the corridor learning the last finer points of this that and the other, and even at the end of it we'd both come off and say "I wasn't happy with that". It got really intense.'

As a former *Blue Peter* presenter, Matt is used to challenging both body and mind. But he admits that even he was surprised by the all-consuming nature of the training and performing.

'You naively go in thinking you're going to do a little bit of dancing, but it does take over your life and it will absorb as much of you as you want to give it, so if you want to train 24 hours a day, then it's there for you. And it's not just the dancing, it takes over your whole brain, your thought process, the way you arrange each day, your eating habits, your fitness level, keeping everything going, thinking about nutrients – everything has to be taken into account and it is a big physical ask.'

And tough cookie Aliona wasn't cutting him any slack. In his third week, she sneaked in a quickstep that would have stumped a *Strictly* champ. 'That was the hardest dance for me and I really struggled with it,' he says. 'Aliona now admits it was actually a professional routine. A lot of quicksteps are bouncy, bouncy but for us it was bang, bang, bang, bang, really fast, and it was a real challenge. That was a breaking point for me. It was three weeks into the series, and that was the point where I knew it was all or nothing so I decided it had to be all.'

Throughout the series Matt was not only working on *Country File*, but guest presenting on *The One Show*, which he now fronts full-time. It meant little time to spend at home with wife Nicola, and children Luke and Molly.

'It was a very difficult time for me in that sense,' he recalls. 'Looking back on it now I don't know how I actually did it. I had incredible support from my family and my wife, Nicola, was absolutely amazing. She was there every Saturday supporting me. She didn't see a lot of me but when she did, it was absolutely perfect.'

And Nicola could offer more practical help than the usual *Strictly* partner.

'I was like a robot at home because I would literally come in, eat, rest and recuperate. But she's a physiotherapist as well, so there was a lot more than just support there, she was actually massaging me and keeping me on my feet, so in more ways than one I couldn't have done it without her.'

With an impressive week 1 score of 31, Matt and Aliona planted their feet firmly in the top four of the leader board, and their score never dipped below that mark. In the nail-biting final Matt battled it out against Pamela and Kara with his sizzling samba, an elegant Viennese waltz, a passionate paso and a showdance that would put most acrobats to shame. Pipped at the post by Kara and Artem, Matt is bearing no grudges.

'I honestly wasn't bothered because I knew I'd given it everything,' he declares. 'It was down to the public and I didn't stand there and think, "I could have gone out there and done this better." Therefore I was really happy with what we'd achieved. Of the three of us there – myself, Pamela and Kara – any of us could have won. All three of us deserved it.

'I have an enormous amount of respect for Pamela. I just hope that when I'm in my sixties I'm like her. I take my hat off to her and I would have loved to have seen her lift the trophy. Equally, I thought Kara was absolutely beautiful. I said in the final that I would have voted for her, and I would have done. She was a joy to watch and I loved watching the pair of them dance. Even on tour, I never lost that. For me it would have been nice to have won but we got to the finish line and I was really happy with that. There was a really good feeling in that final and it didn't feel like we were dancing against each other, it felt like we were dancing for ourselves.'

For Matt the main objective was to push himself as far as he could go, and to show the public a side of him that they had never seen before. 'The outcome at the end of the day was good for me and I had a wonderful experience,' he says. 'As I travel around Britain now I meet so many people who enjoyed watching us and that's all you can ask for. That's what *Strictly* is about. People sit down on a Saturday night, they watch the dancing, they get locked in and they love it. For me to be part of that and to have affected people in the way that we did was enough. It wasn't about picking up a glitterball, it was about giving people a really good show on a Saturday night.'

These days, with *The One Show* keeping him busy, Matt has little time for backflips, cartwheels and somersaults. But his twinkle-toes get the occasional airing in the privacy of his own home.

'My wife and I had a little boogie the other night,' he says. 'We've had an extension done and we've got a big wooden floor down in our kitchen-diner, so we waltzed around there the other. So now I'm starring in *Strictly Kitchen*.'

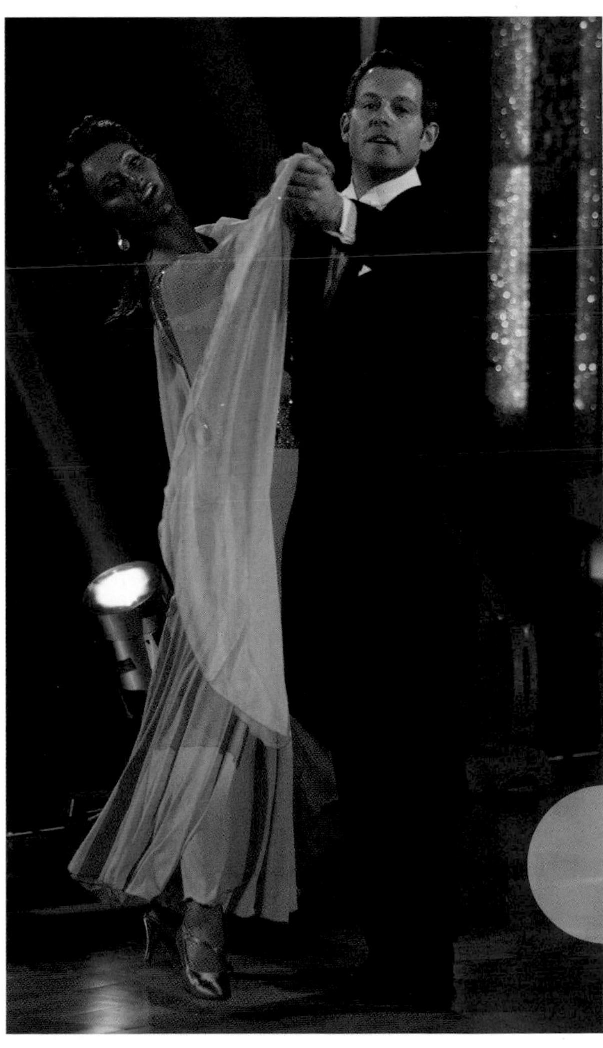

THE LIVE TOUR THE REVEL-UTION

While some of the contestants from *Strictly Come Dancing* are hanging up their Cuban heels and looking forward to a well-earned rest, others are shining their shoes and polishing up their best dances for the Live Tour. The nationwide event is their chance to take the sparkle of *Strictly* to the masses, and the audiences have a whale of a time.

Warm-up man Stuart Holdham, who gets to whip the expectant crowd into a frenzy before the start of the show, says the atmosphere is electric at the arena events. 'It's a totally different atmosphere because we only have a few hundred people in the TV studio, and over a million people applied for tickets, so most people who apply don't get a chance to see it,' he says. 'So when we tour around the country, all these people who watch the show on a Saturday night get to see the people they love face to face.'

The fourth year of the sell-out spectaculars kicked off in January 2011 and stretched over six weeks with performances in Sheffield, Liverpool, Glasgow, Belfast, Birmingham, Manchester, Dublin and London. Competing for the nightly glitterball award were 6 series 8 stars, including winner Kara Tointon and finalists Pamela Stephenson and Matt Baker, along with series 7 runner-up Ricky Whittle and series 3 finalist Colin Jackson. And to tie in with the new-look BBC show, the tour got a makeover from its brand-new director, none other than Craig Revel Horwood. With 30 years of theatrical experience as dancer, choreographer and director, he was the perfect man to add a little razzmatazz to proceedings.

'I wanted to make it as theatrical as possible,' he explains. 'You get to see the singers and get to see the band, and to be introduced to the vocalists. And I put a raised platform in the centre to highlight the dancing because it's a humungous floor on which to perform and some of the dancing, particularly if there's a couple on there, gets lost. I wanted to elevate it, contain it and focus it into one central platform, which splits apart at the end.

'It was a huge challenge for the production team but it works really well because it lights up beautifully and it shows the audience all the footwork. We can use the space around it as well as the space on it. It's a lot more theatrical and a lot more of a show.'

Working closely with *Strictly* Executive Producer Moira Ross, Craig redesigned the set to reflect the changes she had brought to the television series. He copied the purple and silver tones and, as well as the central plinth, he added arches and two huge video screens for the special effects. 'I really loved working with the team and Moira has been absolutely fantastic,' he says. 'We worked together on what sort of music we wanted, running orders and all the details. It's had fantastic reviews and everyone has had a really good time.'

Coming on board as director, as well as judge on the tour, Craig was bursting with ideas but he admits he may have got a bit carried away to begin with. 'I wanted the satellites to split into quarters and go to each quarter of the arena, and then the dancers be hooked up to wires and fly across in a formation,' he laughs, 'I've got a million ideas but unfortunately it would have cost £5.2 million by the time I'd finished with it!'

As well as the financial cost, Craig had the transportation to consider. On the last night at each venue the set has to be dismantled and transported to the next city by the following morning, in order for the team to set it up again for the evening show. The whole set, the lighting, the video screens and the extensive wardrobe is squeezed into five trucks and, while the cast and judges get some well-earned shuteye in their hotel, the production team snooze in hammocks on the tour bus, so that they can be at the venue bright and early the next morning.

Unlike previous tours, the eight competing celebrities were all competent dancers, performing their highest scoring routines from the series. 'We've been really lucky with the amount of talent we've had, because they really are all very good dancers,' says Craig. 'I wanted it to be a fairer competition. I wanted the audience to experience really good dancing all night, not have someone in there as a comedy act.'

Outside of the nightly competition, however, was the best comedy act of all – Craig performing the Charleston with Ann Widdecombe. 'Ann and I come in as a late entry, after the voting closes, so that the audience can have it for their delight – or to throw stones at!'

The act, which begins with the intro to Ann's famous *Titanic* routine, goes down a storm but Craig admits he was initially reluctant to include it.

'Moira came up with the idea of me dancing with Ann and I was horrified, of course,' he recalls. 'Then I thought, actually, that's probably not a bad idea. It's a nice light entertainment button to the evening and then we launch into a big finale.'

BEHIND THE SCENES

5pm | Backstage at the Manchester Evening News Arena, just a few days before the tour ends, the corridors are beginning to buzz with life. The female celebs and dancers are arriving in groups and most head straight to hair and make-up, where the team have their heated tongs and make-up brushes at the ready. Patsy Kensit is having her hair put into rollers and Kara is being filmed for a TV show, while Aliona Vilani, Ola Jordan and Tina O'Brien patiently wait their turn. Tina is visibly excited about the show tonight because Manchester is her home town and a very special guest, two-year-old daughter Scarlett, will be in the audience.

Tina, who is performing the foxtrot and Charleston with series partner Jared Murillo, said that dancing in front of an arena audience of thousands was 'scary', but not a patch on the nerve-jangling build up of a Saturday night in the *Strictly* studio.

'The first live show of *Strictly* was easily the most terrifying experience of my life,' she laughs. 'Every single show I found I would stand backstage and I would literally think, how am I even going to walk down the stairs?. That was really scary but it gives you a new confidence as well because I think if I can do that, I can do anything.'

5.15pm | The bulk of the performers are in the catering area, getting some much needed refuelling before the hard work begins. Matt Baker chats to partner Aliona and Jimi Mistry as they tuck in and they have plenty of praise for the hard-working chefs. 'The food is unbelievable,' says Matt. 'The catering company come with us on tour, and it's never the same twice.'

Before the show begins, Matt and Aliona are on the brink of clinching the record for the most wins on tour. They have already danced their way to victory in 24 of the 28 shows and are nearing Rachel Stevens' precious record of 26.

'We're winning every night and it feels good,' says Aliona. 'Everyone is saying "Come on, when are you going to let someone else win" but we say, "We're just making up for losing *Strictly*." It's all very friendly competition.'

Coming straight from the series, she believes, gives them an advantage over Colin Jackson and Ricky Whittle, the two celebrities from previous years. 'The celebrities who come straight from the show are still in dance mode. It's very hard to get into it again once you've stopped for a while.'

On the opposite side of the table Ann Widdecombe is in deep

conversation with tour presenter Zoe Ball, who is delighted to be back in the *Strictly* fold. 'It's great to be back,' she says. 'The thing is that since I did the series I've become such a *Strictly* fan. I just love it! I did the tour four years ago and I think this tour is just rocking, it's really good.'

Having come third in series 3, Zoe is quite the twinkle-toes herself and she opens the show by dancing with the professionals. Even so, she's relieved she's not competing. 'I dance at the beginning and that's terrifying enough but the standard is so high. I think the standard is so much higher than it was when I took part. Matt and Kara are quite incredible.'

Former MP Ann, who had the nation in stitches during the series, is happy to provide the light entertainment on the tour as well. 'I do feel it's a bit of a cheat because everybody else is doing serious stuff and then Craig and I come on at the end and do a pantomime act, and we get cheered to the rafters,' she marvels. 'I don't dance, Craig dances!' Asked what she thinks of Craig's moves she quips, 'Surprisingly light-footed.'

5.30 pm | Judges Len Goodman, Craig Revel Horwood and Bruno Tonioli are hanging out in their communal dressing room. 'The Three Stooges', as Craig refers to them, provide the vital difference that lifts the live show from dance spectacle to interactive entertainment.

Despite their onscreen rows over the finer points of ballroom, the three men have a ball while on tour. 'It's been great working with Len and Bruno on this and we get on very well backstage. During the tour we've had such a laugh because I'm always looking for bargains in the January sales, so we go from city to city and shop 'til we drop. I've had to buy an extra suitcase to get it all in.'

Effusive Italian Bruno is also enjoying the touring experience and is full of praise for his fellow judges. 'I'm having a fantastic time,' he says. 'We have such a giggle as the judges, and being with Mr Goodman is like a never-ending box of delights – you never know what you are going to get day by day.'

With just a few days left to go, Len admits he'll be sorry to see it end. 'We've had the most marvellous cast of celebrities and professional dancers, the whole atmosphere has been fantastic and I've thoroughly enjoyed it from day one,' he says. 'My only disappointment would be that next Sunday it grinds to a halt, and I've got to go back to my humdrum existence. What a wonderful job Craig Revel Horwood has done. He's really made it into a proper production.'

6.00 pm | The costume department and hair and make-up are kept busy as celebrities and professionals flit in and out completing last-minute preparations. The door to the girls' communal changing room is constantly opening and closing as they dash out for a final adjustment to hair or lipstick.

In the arena, the first of the audience are starting to arrive and their excited chatter fills the bars and lobby. The majority of the fans have dressed up to the nines in glitter, sparkle and lace, in true *Strictly* style, and they are ready to join the party.

Patsy, still in rollers backstage, has been delighted by the fan's reaction to the live shows. 'They are such big arenas and it amazes me the huge turnout in each city,' she says. 'And they're great crowds so, although it's been nerve-racking, it's also fun. The tour is a nice conclusion to the whole *Strictly* experience, a nice way for it to end. It's really been 6 months now, because we started at the end of August and finish in the middle of Feb but I've loved it.'

Patsy admits she was surprised that she stayed in until week 9 on the series and is full of praise for dance partner Robin. 'It was Robin's first year doing it and he's a really lovely man, so I was really lucky.'

Professional partner Robin is used to performing in front of live audiences, having previously starred in *Burn the Floor*, but is still amazed by the audience response. 'It's my first tour and my first year, and it's been an incredible experience from the start right through until now,' he reveals. 'Every city we've been to, it gets better and better.'

6.15 pm | The cast are gathering backstage where Craig gives last-minute directions to the professional dancers. Several of the stars are stretching and warming up in preparation for their dances and a beaming Tina introduces daughter Scarlett to the rest of the gang. Colin, Ricky and James are whiling away the time before the show starts with an on-going *Scrabble* challenge on their smartphones while others chat. Kara and Artem are polishing on their paso doble, which they will dance in the second half and, pep talk over, Craig pirouettes through the performers as he prepares to go on stage. Despite the looming live performance the atmosphere is surprisingly relaxed and easy.

'This is probably the best thing I've ever done for sheer enjoyment factor,' Colin Jackson reveals. For the tour Colin swapped his series 3 partner Erin Boag for Ola Jordan. And with so many changes in the professional dancers' line up, Colin was pleased to be reunited with the three original judges and with his fellow finalist Zoe Ball.

'They made it easy to come back,' he says. 'But I was very rusty. It was probably about six shows into the live tour before I could dance properly. I only had four or five hours to train before the show with a new partner, and I had to learn four dances, because we have the group dance and the finale as well as our own. But when you love something, and you have a passion for something, it's very easy to throw yourself back into it.'

6.30 pm | Showtime! Stuart Holdham has whipped the crowd into a frenzy with his hilarious warm-up routine and the anticipation in the arena is electric. As the dancers limber up backstage, the familiar theme tune is greeted with deafening applause and cheering from the auditorium and Zoe's opening dance – to Shirley Bassey's 'Get This Party Started' goes down a storm.

6.45pm | The show is in full swing and each couple leaving the floor comes to the backstage area buzzing and most head straight to the dressing room to change for their next dance. Colin and Ola have opened the show with a sizzling cha cha cha and the audience are lapping up each dance. Each couple waits in the wings as they prepare to take to the stage and, as in the TV show, their slightly nervous faces are beamed on to the screens in the auditorium. Then the descent down the staircase to the dance floor is replicated, albeit on a bigger scale.

On stage, the central platform is lit by fluorescent lights and the back of the set is flanked by two sweeping staircases and the huge purple arches familiar to viewers of the latest series. A huge glitterball decorates the back, along with mirrors and the two video screens. The judges watch from their table at the side but the audience can also voice their opinions from their seats by waving the banners emblazoned with Craig's catchphrases, 'Dis-ahs-ter' and 'Fab-U-Lous.'

7.30pm | The show breaks for an interval, while the audience relax with a drink, but backstage it is still a hive of activity. The performers rush off to their dressing rooms to change into their costumes for the second half. The hair and make-up artists are now stationed in the cast area, to carry out the quick changes needed between dances, and the female celebs take turns at the table getting the necessary new styles .

7.50 pm | Colin and Ola are first on once again and the 'rusty' athlete trips up the stairway in the quickstep as lightly as a modern-day Fred Astaire. But it doesn't all go according to plan and after the dance he confesses, 'I nearly dropped Ola on her head!' His strict teacher agrees, 'he got told off. I could see in his face, he was thinking what have I done?'

Tina and Jared's foxtrot is a triumph, and Len calls them 'a couple of dancing Munchkins,' before Tina points out her daughter in the audience and gives her a wave. They're followed by Ricky and Natalie, whose tango earns them the second perfect score of the night. After a sexy Argentine tango, Craig tells a thrilled Pamela, 'You've just proved grannies can tango!'

Matt's samba, complete with four backflips, brought the house down and had Bruno declaring, 'Quite a few ladies over there are hyperventilating. I think they need mouth to mouth!' But for reigning champ Kara, things didn't go so well, as she slipped in the American smooth and fell over. 'I didn't think my mum and dad coming was a good idea,' she told the audience. 'You're never coming again. Sorry about the fall.'

8.40 pm | The couples' dances are over and the audience are voting, using their mobile phones. In the meantime, Ann and Craig perform the most entertaining dance of the evening, the Charleston, and get a standing ovation. Matt and Aliona are once more revealed as the winners of the evening, leaving them just one show off the record, which they would go on to equal in Glasgow.

8.55 pm | After a stunning finale with all the dancers and professionals joining in, the show is over for another night. After another standing ovation, the crowd begin to file out, chatting and smiling happily after a great evening's entertainment. A few minutes later, back in ordinary clothes with hairpieces and make-up removed, the performers and judges head back to their hotel to unwind while the production team set about dismantling the set and loading up the trucks.

STRICTLY STYLE ON TOUR

Costumes

Glitter and glamour are as much a part of the Live Tour as the TV show and transferring the distinctive style from screen to stage is the job of designer Victoria Gill and tour wardrobe manager Mo Thompson. In previous years, the dresses worn in the actual series have been sold on by the company that owns them or given away to raise money for charity, but this tour was different.

'For the first time we got some of the costumes from the show because Victoria, who works very closely with dance company DSI, managed to keep a few,' says Mo. 'But the costumes for the TV show only have to do a dress rehearsal and a show whereas ours have to last for six weeks and be worn nearly every night so they need to be a bit harder wearing, a bit sturdier. They are still built in the same way, as leotards with a dress built on top, but they can't be too flimsy.'

Although Victoria works with the dancers throughout the series, Mo only gets to meet them a week before the tour, during the week they are rehearsing in London. For performers and designers alike, it's a busy few days. 'We'll have final fittings there and that's where I meet all the new people who haven't done the tour before,' explains Mo. 'Then I'm involved in getting it all together, packing it up in London and bringing it to the first venue.'

A vital detail of the week is making sure the cast have the correct shoes for their dances.

'They get very attached to their shoes,' says Mo. 'So we have to try and keep them the same. There are different heel heights, different widths, and they have a Latin shoe and a ballroom shoe so there's a lot to analyse there, and the shoes are usually quite a headache.'

When the garments are sourced, sewn, stoned and ready to go, they are packed into flight cases, big enough to hang a full-length gown, and loaded on to the trucks.

'We have 17 flight cases but not all of them are filled with costumes,' she says. 'All the gents' outfits go in one, the ladies' in another, the judges and host go in a third and the band's go in another. We've got three filled with equipment and some other big cases, one of which is filled with spare shoes, another with laundry products. Then there's haberdashery stuff, laundry baskets, ironing boards, coat-hangers – although we've never got enough coat-hangers!'

A lot of the outfits, particularly the men's shirts, have to be washed every night but the more delicate dresses can be spot cleaned. 'We use a non-toxic chemical to spot clean and, as most of the dresses are only on for a couple of minutes, that's enough if you can keep on top of it. We also spray them with vodka. That's what the Russian ballet companies used to do to keep their dresses fresh.'

Although the dresses stay the same throughout the tour, there are still daily repairs and alterations.

'Sometimes you get rips in the hems from girls catching their heels in skirts, and the fabric is quite thin so it can rip easily. We do our best with mending but one of the good things is that even with those big screens, they can't see the costume close up. We might think, oh my God, that looks awful, but on the stage and the screen you can't see it.

'One of the main problems is that the fabrics drop and stretch a lot so something that fitted beautifully at the beginning can get loose, so we have to take things in and take up elastic straps when they stretch. And we have to keep restoning things. The stoning lasts quite well but when we hand-wash things, the stones tend to fall off, so we have a "sparkle drawer" full of stones and glue. There are four of us in the department so two of us start ironing, one will do seaming and one will start on repairs and we kind of rotate to stop it getting boring.'

As well as the costumes, shoes and ironing boards, Mo travels with two washing machines, two tumble dryers and a hot box, where delicate garments that can't be tumble dried can be hung. She also has a spinner for the hand-washed items, at the bottom of which a large handful of crystals lies, having fallen off the gowns in the process.

Talking during the last show at the Manchester venue, Mo has had a relatively relaxed day, starting at 4pm. But with a move to Glasgow on the cards after the show this evening, she has a busy night ahead. She sits in a cavernous and almost empty room, having already unplumbed the washing machines ready to be wheeled out to the trucks, and is still packing away last-minute items as the show goes on.

'Tomorrow we'll start at 9am because it's a loading day, when the show switches venues. I've got to plumb the washing machines in, set up the room, and put all the cases in, set up the rails. We take things into the dressing rooms, make sure there are towels for everybody, get the washing and laundry done, and tackle any repairs.

'Then there are slight alterations. For example Pamela wants a Scottish tartan sash on her white Viennese waltz costume for the Glasgow dates, so we're going to have to stone that tomorrow.'

And as the cast relax at the hotel, Mo will already be on the road to Glasgow.

'We are travelling up tonight on the bus,' she reveals. 'There are four tour buses that take all the crew and we've all got a little bunk that we sleep in. We load all our stuff, then we have a shower in the venue before we leave. There's wine, beer and sandwiches so we eat and have a drink, get into our bunks and wake up in the car park of the next venue and off we go again.'

Hair and Make-up

When it comes to speedy makeovers between dances, Sally O'Neill is a dab hand with the lippy. After coming on board on the very first tour, in 2008, she is used to the quick changes between Latin and ballroom dances and has a few tricks up her sleeve.

'Time is the main challenge,' she explains. 'Everybody comes in at five o'clock and then they've got to eat and get ready, have their hair done etc. There are only five of us on the team so there's quite a lot to get through. But I've done it from the start, as have my colleagues Fran and Tracy, so we're used to it. It ends up a little like driving a car, you know what you're doing without thinking. The first show is the hardest because you're establishing the order but once everybody's happy it all runs smoothly.'

Like Mo, Sally meets the celebrities about a week in advance and then goes through their costumes to decide on the look for the live show. The fact that they have all been through the series first means that most of the celebrities already have a good idea about their own look. 'The girls tend to know what's going to work and whether they want their hair up or down because they know what the dances are like and how fast they are,' says Sally. 'Because of the quick turnaround we tend to do lip changes more than eye-colour changes.'

When the eyeshadow shades and hairstyles are chosen, each performer has a cosmetics bag of their own, so the make-up is not mixed up, and the team transport everything from venue to venue, including mirrors and lights.

'We have three flight cases which are about ten foot by five, then there are the mirrors and we carry a lot of lights as well because some of the dressing rooms aren't properly lit.'

As well as the vast array of make-up, curling tongs and rollers set out in the dressing room, there are a number of wigs and hairpieces, an essential part of the tour wardrobe. 'The first thing we do at each venue is set the hairpieces,' reveals Sally. 'They all use them, no matter how long or short their hair, because five weeks of putting constant heat on to someone's hair will ruin it. So to save time we use wigs and hairpieces and preset everything. Their hair is underneath, scraped back in a ponytail.'

As if to prove the point, Kara arrives with her hair scraped back and is given an change of style, from Latin to ballroom, in seconds. A steady stream of stars that follow for an instant makeover in the backstage beauty parlour, and the efficiency and speed would put most salons to shame. But Sally takes it all in her stride.

'It's all organised so that everybody knows exactly what they're doing before the tour starts,' she says. 'We're all used to it now.'

Anita Dobson

Whether she proves a dancer or a dis-ah-ster, no one can accuse Anita Dobson of lacking enthusiasm. The former EastEnder is lapping up the Latin and having a ball with the Ballroom, and even at the end of a hard day's training she can't contain her glee.

'I'm just loving it!' she gushes. 'I've always wanted to learn ballroom dance, so it's just brilliant to finally be doing it. I'm so full of the whole experience. I love it totally, unreservedly, 100 per cent. I'm not here to be the best, I'm not into showing off. I'm just here to enjoy it.'

Anita was born in the East End and took up acting as a child. At 21, she was accepted into the Webber Douglas School of Singing and Dramatic Art and, after leaving, quickly found jobs in television programmes *Up the Elephant and Round the Castle* and *Play Away*. In 1985, she became the first landlady of the Queen Vic when she landed the role of Angie Watts. The emotional rollercoaster of her marriage to 'Dirty Den' enthralled the nation and, in 1986, the couple starred in the highest rated soap episode ever, when 30 million people tuned in to watch her errant husband hand Angie divorce papers on Christmas Day.

Away from the screen, Anita is happily married to Queen guitarist Brian May. But she reveals he had his reservations about her *Strictly* adventure. 'Brian was a bit nervous because it takes over your life and it's full on, and I think he was worried he wouldn't see much of me. But he's really behind it now. He says, "I've never seen anything bring you so much joy apart from acting, so go for it!"'

And younger sister Gill is over the moon. 'She's retired and she goes to line dancing and zumba classes a few times a week, so the fact that I'm doing *Strictly*, which she watches avidly, means she's so excited you wouldn't believe it.'

While many training sessions are punctuated with tears and tantrums, the bubbly 62-year-old reckons her time with Robin is pure, unadulterated fun.

> I've always wanted to learn ballroom dance, so it's just brilliant to finally be doing it

'He is fantastic,' she reveals. 'Boy did I get lucky! He's adorable. He's a lovely guy and he's also a very good teacher. I understand where he's coming from. We love the same things, we have fun, which I think is crucial with dance, especially if you're learning. If you're not having fun then really, you shouldn't do it. At the same time, he pushes me a little bit further every day and gives me something else to think about. I couldn't have asked for a better partner.'

Despite her obvious enjoyment, Anita admits to an attack of nerves before the launch show and has vowed she won't let fear get in her way again. 'I got myself in a terrible state because I went into the studio and met up with the rest of the group, and everybody was talking about their experience of training so I started to get really wound up. But then I said to myself, if you stay this wound up you're not going to enjoy it. Put the nerves to one side and just do it. Now I'm much more relaxed and focussed. I'm not worrying about what the end result is going to be because it won't solve anything. Worry gets you nowhere.'

Dan Lobb

D*aybreak* presenters Kate Garraway and Christine Bleakley have both taken to the floor on the show, with mixed results, and now it's the turn of co-host Dan Lobb. Kate was kept in until week 7, despite consistently low scores, while Christine made it through to the quarter finals. GMTV stars Fiona Phillips and Andrew Castle also possessed two left feet.

'I know Kate loved the experience but the GMTV faces didn't have the greatest success, so I do feel I am carrying the hopes of the station as well as the programme,' says Dan. 'I hope I can do them proud.'

But the tennis pro turned sports presenter did get a little bit of a pep talk from Christine. 'She's warned me that it's really hard work and if you're not careful it will take over your life, but she is very complimentary about the show and the production in general and she said it was something I should do and that I'd never regret it.'

Dan Lobb grew up just outside Winchester in Hampshire and studied Biology, Chemistry and Economics before accepting a tennis scholarship to the University of Tennessee. After graduating he played on the professional tennis circuit for 3 years, reaching a British ranking of 18, and after retiring in 1998 he went on to coach. Four years later he landed a job on Sky Sports News and, in May 2009, Lobb became a sports presenter on Sky News. Joining GMTV in 2010, Dan became sports editor when he switched to the ITV's new morning show *Daybreak*.

Paired with Katya for the show, Dan has been fitting training hours around his job. 'Katya understands that I can't devote all day every day,' he explains. 'I have a fulltime job and I'm up at 3.30 in the morning so she has to work around that. But Katya's very driven and she knows what she wants and how to get the best out of me. I don't think she would be doing her job if she wasn't pushing me but she's not going overboard and I don't think she could.'

Ballroom dancing is alien to me. It's not an extension to the kind of dad dancing that I have done round the dance floors of the United Kingdom

The 39-year-old admits he likes a little boogie on a night out, but says it's a world away from what he is learning now. 'I have natural rhythm but I'm not a natural dancer,' he admits. 'Ballroom dancing is alien to me. It's not an extension to the kind of dad dancing that I have done round the dance floors of the United Kingdom. We are learning a brand new skill from scratch. It's difficult, challenging, rewarding in equal measure and it's fun in places too!'

Although he is used to the TV cameras, Dan confesses to terrible nerves on the night of the launch show. 'It's very weird for me to be in a television studio in that kind of environment without being the presenter, not having an idea of the rundown, the scripts and everything. But the whole thing was nerve-racking in itself because you're out on show for the first time, and we were building up to the group dance at the end which we were all really scared about. It was a great day and a great evening but we all breathed a huge sigh of relief when it was all done.'

Bruno's Hotlist

Bruno Tonioli had plenty of reasons to leap out of his chair and fling his arms around during the last series of *Strictly*. And if sex kitten Kara, acrobat Matt and hot-to-trot Ssssscott weren't enough to get the excitable Italian fired up there was the outrageous kiss from rugby hunk Gavin Henson.

'The line-up for series eight was great,' he says. 'We had such a wonderful mixture of characters, which made it more interesting. And it wasn't just the more mature ladies, like Felicity and Pamela, but we had a few young hunks, like lovely Ssssscott and Gavin. They were very competitive and for me it was the best *Strictly* so far.'

Not all the mature ladies came in for praise and Bruno had some choice words for politician Ann Widdecombe, comparing her to a 'Dalek in drag', 'E.T's mum' and 'Vera Duckworth's grandmother in the Great Depression.' And he was booed by the audience when he told partner Anton, 'You must have a slipped disc the way he was swinging you around.'

Secretly, however, he admits he is a bit of an Ann fan. She's great. 'She's such a nice lady, who I got to know much better on tour,' he recalls. 'During the series I don't have much time to mingle with the celebrities, as I am also doing the American show. But she was really a lovely lady, very smart, very funny, very professional. She was great for the show and great to have on tour.' Here's Bruno's take on series eight.

What did you think of the series 8 final?

It was brilliant, really good. They were all good and they all did excellent dances and Kara was just stunning. I know she did the last two dances with an injury but she and Artem were amazing together, with so much chemistry. Physically they match each other, she's got a great body for dancing and the routines looked stunning. Incredible. They all did well and it was a very, very good show. It was a deserved win.

Who surprised you the most?

I thought Pamela was very, very good. She didn't crack, she was very brave and she danced beautifully, and never for a moment played the old woman. She worked as hard as anybody else and did incredibly well, and that's what's so good about the show – the unpredictability of it.

Who disappointed you?

I know how difficult ballroom and Latin are so you can't really say anybody is surprisingly bad. I've done enough shows now to know that anything can happen and you can never predict. Inevitably there are people who are young and funky who can do well, but they all have to put the work in to it.

Who improved the most?

I think Gavin improved, bless him. He started pretty tragically and it took him a while to get going but once he started to take his clothes off he somehow increased in confidence. Patsy Kensit improved a lot too, but with her it was just nerves. When she conquered her nerves she actually started to get better, and began to look good because confidence and technique work together.

'You got the wrong song. It should have been Could It Be Tragic!'

Did anyone go too soon?
Goldie deserved another chance and Jimi went out quite early. I was very surprised. Jimi had a few weeks left in him but then again, it's down to the public vote. It really didn't reflect the judges' vote when he went. He had some problems but everyone had problems to start with, and he was doing well. It happens, and that's the way it works. Sometimes when we get about halfway through the public assume that people are safe, and then they don't vote for them and that's when the upsets happen. It happens every year in the middle of the series. Someone like Jimi is in the middle of the table so they vote for the ones at the bottom and someone who is a better dancer goes out.

Favourite dance of the series?
Kara's American smooth which she did in Blackpool and the final. It was really something, created a great atmosphere and the music was great. It was very original, the way the whole thing was put together. It had drama, which is often missing in the American smooth, it had the impact of a paso doble, and beautiful choreography. It was stunning. Artem did a really good job. He came in very strong, so he was a very good addition to the show.

Did you miss the dance off?
The dance off always gave us a few problems, because everyone ended up blaming the judges even though the last two were down to the public vote at the end of the day. With the dance off we could never win because we have to get rid of one, and obviously 50 per cent of the audience are going to be rooting for that person, so whatever we did we were wrong. I think there were more problems than advantages with it, from my point of view. We do our job, we express our opinions and you may or may not agree with us, but at the end of the day the public lend their voice and the dance off was a way of adding something that wasn't necessary. We do the show for the public and I totally agree that if the people want Ann Widdecombe to keep doing what she was doing, that's fine for me. I never had a problem with that – it's the nature of the show.

What did you think of the new set?
It's fantastic, it's wonderful. It has a real Hollywood feel, evoking the 1930s, Fred and Ginger. The arches and the slight Art Deco line looked brilliant. It really enhanced the glamour of the show and gave it a much more sleek and polished look.'

Are you expecting more drama and theatrics this year?
That's very much a production decision but the props and backdrops helped set up the mood for the performance and I think it went down so well last year. If something works, we don't want to mess with it. I get the feeling there will be more of the same this year. It would be crazy to change it.

Bruno's Best Bits:

On Paul and Ola's week one cha cha cha to 'Could it be Magic'.
'You got the wrong song. It should have been Could It Be Tragic!'

After Ann Widdecombe's week 1 waltz
'It was like watching the Ark Royal taking on the stormiest of seas. The ride was bumpy but you made it in to port.'

After Scott's week 3 quickstep
'Ssssscott, that was an action-packed adventure of a quickstep. It was Indiana Scott in the Temple of Dance.'

On Peter's week 4 Charleston
'You looked like a penguin stuck in the mud: You couldn't quite get going.'

After Jimi's Hallowe'en paso doble, to Michael Jackson's 'Thriller'
'You obviously love being the flesh-eating living dead. You dance better as the living dead than you ever have before. Stay in character, love.'

On Pamela's week 6 foxtrot.
'Pamela goes to Hollywood. The glamour of Marilyn, the equipment of Jane Mansfield and the dancing ability of Ginger Rogers.'

Chelsee Healey

Being partnered with new boy Pasha Kovalev has its benefits for contestant Chelsee Healey. 'We've both got to prove ourselves because nobody's seen him dance yet, as he's new to the series, so that takes some of the pressure off me. He's a beautiful person and he's a great teacher, he's absolutely brilliant. I couldn't ask for a better teacher.'

Even so, the 23-year-old actress admits the training has come as a shock and, fitting sessions around a full-time job filming *Waterloo Road*, has proved tough. Even before the first show, she was reduced to tears by sheer fatigue. 'I never thought it was going to be this hard,' she reveals. 'In the first week I was in tears because I'm so hard on myself. If I can't get something right, I take it personally. It just got to me a bit because I'd been up since 6am with *Waterloo Road* and I was really tired.'

Grabbing rehearsal time when she's not filming means the sociable actress has very little spare time. 'In between scenes I'm just trying to get as much rest as I can. Then after I finish I'm straight on to rehearsal, then get a good night's sleep. But some weeks I'm not filming so I can train all day, which is good. I don't mind the lack of free time. I like to put the work in!'

Chelsee was born and bred in Eccles, near Manchester, and made her screen debut at the age of 15, playing Katie Moore in the series *Burn It*. Guest appearances in such shows as *Two Pints of Lager and a Packet of Crisps*, *Doctors* and *Hollyoaks* followed and, in 2006, she landed the role of cheeky schoolgirl Janeece Bryant in the school drama *Waterloo Road*. After three years as a pupil, Chelsee's character left the school, only to return as the new secretary in the following series.

This year's youngest contestant follows in the dainty footsteps of her co-star, Tina O'Brien, who made it to week 5 in the last series. 'Tina just said, "Good luck. And have an amazing time," which was nice,' she says. 'She was poorly with chicken pox during the show but she did the tour and said she had the best time ever.'

A big fan of *Strictly*, Chelsee says she signed up for the show because, 'I thought it would be fun. I've not danced properly since I was a baby, so it would be a bit of a challenge, and I just love to watch the show so I thought it would be a great experience. I used to do ballet and tap until I was about 12 years old, when I got my first acting jobs. But I don't think that will help because it's not ballet or tap, it's ballroom so it's very out of my comfort zone.'

I love sparkles so I can't wait to try them on and wear them through the weeks, as long as I'm not out in week 1.

While she is 'dreading' the first live show, there is one aspect of *Strictly* that Chelsee is very much looking forward to – the glamorous outfits.

'The costumes are all amazing,' she says. 'I love sparkles so I can't wait to try them on and wear them through the weeks, as long as I'm not out in week 1. That will be lovely.'

Harry Judd

Drummer Harry knew exactly what he was letting himself in for when he signed up for the show. Unlike the other competitors, he had a taste of *Strictly* fever when he took part in a special episode for Children in Need in 2010. Dancing the paso doble with Ola Jordan, he beat The Saturdays' Rochelle Wiseman to the trophy.

'On reflection I enjoyed it,' he recalls. 'It was really stressful at the time but once you've done it, it's quite satisfying so I thought I'd give it another go.'

But he's adamant the winning performance won't give him an edge on the others.

'I don't think it gives me a head start,' he insists. 'I think there are people in the series who have had a whole lifetime of experience of dancing and then there are people on the show who have never danced, so I may have the advantage over some, but a lot of people have an advantage over me.'

At 17, after seeing an ad in the *New Musical Express*, Harry auditioned to become the drummer for new band McFly. Despite forgetting his drumsticks, he was hired and quickly found fame when the debut single, '5 Colours in Her Hair', and album, *Room on the 3rd Floor*, went straight to number one. A self-taught musician, he can feel the beat but reckons he is far from a natural dancer.

'It helps that I have rhythm but I have to move my whole body this time, not just my arms,' he says. 'The other guys in the band have their guitars but they still throw some shapes around the stage. Not me.'

The Essex-born star has thrown himself into training with partner Aliona Vilani, and admits he finds it tricky to learn the steps.

'We're trying to do as many hours as possible – I need it,' he says. 'It takes a while to go in! Aliona's a tough teacher but she has to be because it is really hard. She has to be very patient and strict with me, and she's great. The professional dancers seem to have the power of patience. Aliona probably just wants to come into work and just start dancing, whereas she has to watch and wait and tell me what to do.'

Aliona's a tough teacher but she has to be because it is really hard. She has to be very patient and strict with me, and she's great.

Away from the training room, the 25-year-old popstar has the support of long-term girlfriend Izzy. And he's hoping his *Strictly* experience will mean he can impress her on the dance floor.

'She's very supportive and she gave me the confidence to do it, because I was quite scared,' he admits. 'She said, "just go for it." She's a good little mover so hopefully I'll be able to throw some shapes with her after this experience.'

But he's expecting a mixture of encouragement and mockery from bandmates Dougie, Tom and Danny. 'They are excited about watching me, and having a good old chuckle at me trying to dance,' he laughs. 'They've been supportive, but at the same time I'm sure they'll have a cheeky dig at me.'

No doubt an army of female fans will be tuning in to watch the pop pin-up strut his stuff in those revealing Latin outfits. And Harry promises a few treats when it comes to the wardrobe.

'The costumes help you get into the character and get into the dance, so it's all part of the fun of the show,' he explains. 'I will be fully embracing that side of it.'

Craig Meets his Match

When Tess asked Craig Revel Horwood if he had been sharpening his claws, at the start of series eight, he quipped, 'No, but I put my tongue in for a service.' Indeed, the celebrities are used to receiving a tongue lashing from the forthright judge but this time one formidable lady was biting back. And after 40 years in the gladiatorial atmosphere of the House of Commons, Ann Widdecombe had learned to fight dirty. Before Craig could even critique her disastrous salsa, she told him, 'Don't bother. You haven't got a zero so give us one and be done with it.' And when he accused her off spending most of the paso doble sitting on her backside, she retorted, 'What do you do all day? You get paid for sitting on your backside.'

The Aussie judge got his own back with a few caustic comments and his lowest marks ever, but he admits he enjoyed every minute. 'I loved it!' he laughs. 'I like people who answer back. The funny thing about Ann is that she'd always anticipate what she thought I was going to say and it was always wrong, so that was quite amusing. She tried to put herself down in the same way I would critique someone's dancing, and that was unusual. Generally you have banter but this was different, and funny. But it's not my fault she can't dance!'

Rather more to his taste was the fab new set. With a long career as a stage dancer and choreographer, the dramatic new look appealed to Craig's theatrical sensibilities. 'I love the colours of it, the purple and silver, because they're much more now,' he says. 'I love the curves. I liked the way it harks back to the 1930s but doesn't actually replicate it entirely. I like the electronic nature of it because it was more space age, bringing the show into the future. It opened the studio out, it fits more audience in which is always good, and I really like Tess's level being part of the whole fabric of the furniture rather than being slung out the back in a two foot square black hole. It was much more glamorous and better for the audience because they could now see what used to happen backstage. It also provided a delicious staircase to walk down.'

Did you miss the dance off?

No. I didn't miss the dance off. I like having it, because we can make a decision and it empowers the judges a little bit more. It gives us the final say on which one of the two couples should go, and generally we all agree and the best dancer goes through, so it was a way of saving the best dancer from the public vote. But without it, it still worked, and it proved that in the end the audience made the right decisions and that they can now make educated choices because there has been eight series, so people are more dance savvy nowadays.

Was Kara a deserving winner?

Kara was always a frontrunner because technically she's the best overall, plus she's very young and very beautiful. Also she had an immaculate story, in that she fell in love on the show, and she's an actress so she can act through the dancing. She wasn't without flaw, however, and Pamela Stephenson was a very equal contender. A lot of people who were Pamela's age were voting for her because when you consider that Pam is in her sixties and so is Ann, the chalk and cheese of it was wonderful. To see someone come through on their journey and losing weight and getting better was fabulous. But Kara deserved to win.

Did the right dancers get into the final?

The top four, after Gavin went, were definitely the best four dancers of the competition so the audience certainly got it right for series 8. They left Ann in for as long as they could stomach and then they really wanted a dance competition at the end, with their favourites so it really was competitive. The final was electric, anything could happen. And Kara injured her arm doing that walkover at the end of her show dance and that hampered her next dance. Matt was determined to win but his show dance was more of gymnastics routine, which was all very spectacular but the majority of viewers, I think, like to see more dance than tricks.

'I only have three letters, my love. OMG!'

Who else impressed you?
Felicity Kendal was great, Patsy Kensit was great at times, Pamela and Kara were fabulous. Tina O'Brien was a little bundle of joy, very sweet, but her dancing sort of replicated that. It was a very musical theatre performance, although she did win a few hearts and she and Jared were a nice combination as the cute couple.

Who left too soon?
Jimi Mistry went out way too early because I know he had more to give but the problem was that he wasn't technically as good as some, like Matt, and he wasn't as competitive as the rest of them. It does, in the end, become a competition and people forget that. They pretend that they're just having a great time and they're all pally and matey but it does get cut-throat as the final looms. Jimi didn't have that competitive nature and he wasn't as naturally gifted as Matt, who really wanted to win.

Why was Goldie first to go?
I really liked Goldie. I don't think Goldie had a problem with the dance. He needed the audience vote but unfortunately the audience didn't vote.

Who was the biggest surprise?
The best surprise was Anton Du Beke and the way he treated Ann Widdecombe. I thought it was clever for him not to let her feet touch the ground, it was clever of him to do the bizarre comedy lifts and clever of him to treat every dance as a bit of a story. They dressed her particularly well, for all of that, and it was good comedy. And she stayed in for ten weeks, which is quite extraordinary for someone who was hopeless at dancing.

Any disappointing dancers?
I thought Gavin Henson would be better than he was. I was really surprised how stiff he was. He had a beautiful face, a beautiful body, everything there to make a dance look great but he just could not do it. Michelle Williams was a big surprise, a big let-down! She wasn't good at all. I thought she was going to be hot to trot but she was a real disappointment. You'd have thought after being in Destiny's Child she would be a great dancer. She had rhythm but the problem was that it wasn't applied to the music properly. She was OK when she was being led around but she was a bit naked in the Latin dances. It was all very stick insect like.

Favourite dance of the series?
Scott's jive. It was incredible because we didn't expect it. We thought it was going to be really bad, and it was really good. The anticipation of a dance is the key, and the jive is always hard so not many people have been able to do it. Jill Halfpenny's was the only other memorable jive, other than the really bad ones, but Scott's was wonderful. It was so entertaining I just enjoyed it, and I found I wasn't looking at it technically because I got carried away just watching him. Natalie is one of the best choreographers, and very talented, and Scott was a fabulous dancer.

The worst dance of the series?
Ann's Charleston that wasn't a Charleston, because she was kissing my photograph, which was repulsive!

Craig's candid quotes:

On Ann's week 1 Waltz
'It was all a bit local authority, darling.'

On Gavin getting the guns out in his week 2 salsa
'Three fundamental flaws – timing, rhythm and hips. If people were voting at home for abdominals, darling, I'm sure you'd win the entire programme but it is about dancing as well.'

To Kara, after her week 3 quickstep
'Cartwheel in heels – I've done that myself darling, and I know how tough that is.'

On Gavin's week 3 rumba
'My floorboards at home have more movement than that. Emotionless, cold, at times vacuous.'

To Pamela and James after their week 6 foxtrot
'The end had more cheese than a Swiss fondue.'

On Ann's week 5 paso doble
'I only have three letters, my love. OMG!'

THE Strictly NIGHT IN

THE *Strictly* NIGHT IN

Saturday is *Strictly* for fun so why not make it party night at your house? That way you can have a sizzling shindig without missing your favourite show. Invite your most glamorous friends and opt for a *Strictly* sparkly dress code. Use tinsel and foil to jazz up the house, turn the lights down low or invest in a disco ball light that will throw different colours around the room. Then kick things off with our scrumptious snacks and super smoothies.

This section includes recipes for *Strictly* themed nosh, plus a roulette game to be played while the main show is on. As an added bonus, you could nominate a judges' catchphrase or event for each person watching, and give them a small prize or a chocolate treat if it is included in the show. For example, one player would have 'Len say "Se-VEN"', another, 'Craig says "Fab-U-lous"' and another 'Alesha awards a 10.'

Whether the evening is for four or forty, you're bound to get a perfect score from your friends for your *Strictly* night in. Let's get the party started!

the Menu

SAMBA SKEWERS AND SIZZLING SALSA

Get started with Latin-inspired juicy, grilled prawn skewers and a veggie-packed hot dip with healthy dippers

* * *

AMERICAN SMOOTH-IES

Low-fat and refreshing, these fruity mocktails are bursting with raspberries and mint and topped off with ginger ale

* * *

CHA CHA CHA-GRILLED CHICKEN WRAPS

Packed with protein, serve these Latino wraps with a fresh green salad. Put all the fillings into bowls on the table and invite your guests to roll their own for a relaxed main course

* * *

STAR-STUDDED TANGO-PASSION SORBETS

Make these ballroom-inspired sorbets the night before, so you can quickly serve up during dances. For added 'sparkle', decorate with a slice of star fruit. This fruity dessert will certainly tango with your taste buds.

SAMBA SKEWERS

SERVES 6, READY IN 35 MINUTES

400g king prawns
1 tbsp harissa paste
zest 1 lemon, juice ½ lemon, plus extra wedges to serve
2 crushed garlic cloves
1 tbsp chopped flat leaf parsley
6 wooden skewers

1 Soak the wooden skewers in water for 30 minutes so that they don't burn while the prawns are cooking. While the skewers are soaking, put the prawns in a dish. Mix together the harissa, lemon zest and juice, garlic and parsley and some seasoning. Gently stir in the prawns so they are completely coated in the marinade, and set aside for 15 minutes.

2 Heat the grill. Thread the prawns on to 6 wooden skewers or 12 mini wooden skewers. Arrange the skewers on a baking tray, brushing over any leftover marinade from the dish. Grill for about 5 minutes, turning, until the prawns turn pink and char at the edges. Serve with extra lemon wedges for squeezing over.

SIZZLING SALSA

SERVES 6, READY IN 25 MINUTES

2 red peppers
2 red chillies
2 tbsp rice wine vinegar
1 tbsp olive oil
1 tsp yellow mustard seeds
2 spring onions, finely sliced
handful coriander leaves, roughly chopped
pinch sugar, to taste

TO SERVE
Cucumber sticks and chicory leaves, for scooping

1 Heat the grill, then grill the peppers and chillies, turning, until the skin is blackened. As each is ready transfer to a bowl, and when all are done, cover with clingfilm and leave to cool.

2 Peel the skin off the peppers and chillies and remove the seeds (remember to wash your hands after handling the chillies). First put one of the peppers and one of the chillies in a food processor with the vinegar and oil and whizz to a purée. Chop the remaining pepper and chilli and then stir into the purée with the mustard seeds and most of the spring onions and coriander. Season with a pinch of sugar, if you need to. Scatter with remaining spring onions and coriander leaves, and serve with cucumber sticks and chicory leaves for scooping.

AMERICAN SMOOTH-IES

SERVES 6, READY IN 10 MINUTES

300g frozen raspberries, defrosted
juice 3 limes
1 tbsp sugar
750ml bottle ginger ale
handful mint leaves and ice cubes, to serve

Whizz the raspberries, lime juice and sugar together in a blender or food processor to a puree. Press the puree through a sieve to remove the seeds. Divide between 6 glasses, add some ice cubes and mint to each one, then top up each with a splash of ginger ale. Add straws or sparkly swizzle sticks to decorate, if you like!

CHA-CHA-CHARGRILLED CHICKEN WRAPS

SERVES 6, READY IN 60 MINUTES

4 skinless chicken breasts
1 tbsp olive oil
2 tbsp fat-free natural yogurt
1 tsp ground cumin
1 tsp ground coriander
1 tsp turmeric
½ x 400g can refried beans
200g can kidney beans, rinsed and drained
6-12 chappatis, or small wholemeal or seeded wraps

FOR THE MINTY YOGURT

200ml pot fat-free natural yogurt
2 tbsp chopped mint
1 tsp white wine vinegar
1 tsp sugar

FOR THE PICKLED ONIONS

1 large, or 2 small red onions, thinly sliced
2 tbsp white wine vinegar
1 tbsp sugar
1 tsp toasted cumin seeds

1 Slash the chicken breasts a little, then mix together the olive oil, yogurt, ground cumin, coriander and turmeric with a little ground pepper. Rub all over the chicken breasts and leave to marinate while you get everything else ready.

2 For the minty yogurt mix together the yogurt, chopped mint, vinegar and sugar and season with a little black pepper. For the pickled onions mix together the sliced red onions, vinegar, sugar and cumin seeds and season with a little salt. Roughly mash the refried beans with the kidney beans and heat in a small pan.

3 Heat the grill. Arrange the chicken breasts on a baking tray and grill for 5–8 minutes on each side until cooked through. Heat the chappatis or wraps according to pack instructions.

4 Slice the chicken breasts into strips. To serve pop everything into bowls and let everyone help themselves – try spreading some beans on a wrap, topping with a few chicken slices, some pickled onions and a dollop of yogurt before rolling up.

STAR-STUDDED TANGO-PASSION SORBETS

SERVES 6, READY IN 25 MINS, PLUS FREEZING

3 ripe mangoes, peeled, stoned and flesh roughly chopped
6 ripe passionfruits
juice ½ lemon
100g caster sugar
200ml water
2–3 star fruit thinly sliced, to serve

1 Start this sorbet the day before to allow time for freezing. Put the mango flesh in a food processor or blender. Halve 4 of the passionfruits, scrape the insides into a sieve held over the mangoes and rub as much as you can of the pulp through with the back of the wooden spoon. Discard the seeds, and whizz the mango and passionfruit pulp to a puree.

2 Put the lemon juice, sugar and water in a pan and heat gently until the sugar has melted. Stir in the puree and cool.

3 Once cool, churn in an icecream machine, following the manufacturer's instructions, then freeze until solid. Or freeze until solid, then quickly break up, whizz briefly back in the blender or food processor again (you may need to do this in batches), then freeze again until solid.

4 To serve, scoop into small bowls, adding a few slices of star fruit if you want, then drizzle with a little passionfruit pulp from the remaining passionfruits.

GAMES TO *play*

Strictly Roulette

ADD A LITTLE EXTRA SPICE to your *Strictly* evening with our fun roulette game. You will need 20 different coloured counters or coins for each player, plus some for the banker. If you haven't got counters, you can cut up some card and mark them with a felt tip.

You will be betting on the judges' individual and collective score for each dance. Place your bets on the numbers between 1 and 40. The banker will pay out evens for the individual score and quadruple the stake for the collective score. You may also bet on odds and evens, 10–19, 20–29 and 30–40 for the collective score only, and the banker will double your stake if you get it right.

So place your bets now!

1–19	1	2	3	4	
	5	6	7	8	
	9	10	11	12	
	13	14	15	16	
	17	18	19	20	20–29
	21	22	23	24	
	25	26	27	28	
30–40	29	30	31	32	
	33	34	35	36	
	37	38	39	40	

Edwina Currie

In previous series, injuries have proved a hindrance to some celebrity dancers. But Edwina Currie decided to join the show in order to recover from a broken ankle. The former cabinet minister slipped on the stairs and broke two bones in January 2011 and had to have several pins inserted into her leg.

'I spent weeks in plaster and then I was hobbling around, quite lame and worried about it,' she explains. 'When the invitation came I thought, maybe the dance practice will get my leg up and in good working order again. But I also accepted partly because there's a moment during any injury when a person feels very down. I've been there, and I thought if somebody else sees me dancing, maybe they'll feel they can get up and join an exercise class or a dance class and get themselves fit and well again while having a lot of fun.'

Ironically, the accident happened as she was on her way to watch a dance performance in Liverpool. 'I was planning to take my little granddaughter, who is five, to see her first ballet,' she recalls. 'The ballet was *The Nutcracker*, but it wasn't the nuts that cracked it was my ankle. I slipped on a flight of steps in the city centre. What tickles me is that people in the South always asked me if I did it skiing, people in the North asked if I was drunk!'

Liverpool-born Edwina studied Chemistry at Oxford University and Economic History at the London School of Economics before going into politics. Elected as a Conservative MP in 1983, she served 14 years in the Commons, including a stint as health minister during which she caused controversy by stating that most UK egg production was 'affected with salmonella,' a statement that was later vindicated. Since leaving politics Edwina has enjoyed a successful career in broadcasting and has written numerous books. In 1999, she married second husband John Jones, a retired detective she met when he was the guest on her radio show.

For her *Strictly* stint she is taking inspiration from two of the contestants from last year – former Tory colleague Ann Widdecombe and finalist Pamela Stephenson.

I'm the oldest member of the group and I believe very strongly that we mature ladies are in our prime, we should not give up, go home and put on our slippers

'I'm the oldest member of the group and I believe very strongly that we mature ladies are in our prime, we should not give up, go home and put on our slippers,' she says. 'Pamela was fabulous. Everybody compares me with Ann, but Pamela would be my dream, to be able to dance as well as her. She was radiant.

'I haven't spoken to Ann but I read an article in which she said the best approach to *Strictly* is "unrelieved jollity." That's certainly going to be my mantra. It's got to be fun. The training is very hard work so if it's not fun, you have to ask yourself why you're doing it.'

Edwina, 64, is dancing with Vincent Simone and has warned him to leave her bad ankle alone. 'I've said to Vincent "You're not going to swing me round by that ankle. I'll swing you round by yours." He had a glint in his eye when I said that.'

She is thriving under the tutelage of the Italian professional who, she says, 'is a very good teacher. He's patient, he doesn't ask too much but he pushes you.' And she is unfazed by his legendary flirting.

'I'm probably of an age to be his mother,' she laughs. 'So when it's hands on, we put our hands in the correct places. No problem.'

Jason Donovan

After an 18 month stint in drag for *Priscilla Queen of the Desert The Musical*, Jason is used to glitz and glamour. But while he's embracing the sequins and heels, getting his top off is not on his wish list.

'I'm not Gavin Henson!' he laughs. 'I'm a 43-year-old father of three. But after *Priscilla*, these costumes are going to be pretty mild. Even the loincloth I wore for *Joseph and the Amazing Technicolor Dreamcoat* was a little more risqué than anything the BBC costume department are likely to come up with.'

Even so, Jason is looking forward to the Latin dances so he can shake his booty. 'For a man who never moves his hips, I'm thoroughly enjoying that aspect,' he says. And he is getting on beautifully with partner Kristina Rihanoff – although he's being careful not to get on the wrong side of boyfriend Joe Calzaghe.

Australian Jason began his acting career at the age of eleven, and found his big break when he was cast as Scott Robinson in *Neighbours*, in 1986. His romance with Kylie Minogue, on and off the screen, led to his first UK number one, the duet *Especially For You* in 1988. Jason left acting to concentrate on his pop career, scoring two more number ones and a hit album, *Ten Good Reasons* the following year.

In 1991, Jason changed direction when he was offered the lead in *Joseph* at the London Palladium, beginning a sellout two year stint. Since then he has starred in many hit shows, including *Chitty Chitty Bang Bang, The Sound of Music* and *Sweeney Todd.*

Although he doesn't believe his musical theatre career will help him with the ballroom, he admits that years of performing in front of a live audience is a bonus. 'I've done a number of shows that I've danced in but I'm not a dancer,' he explains. 'It's not my comfort zone. Out of the three – acting, singing and dancing – it's my least accomplished area, and I've never had formal training. The biggest misconception is that because I'm in musical theatre, dancing is part of my talent but that is not the case. But the timing is good because I've just come out of a show and I don't think I've ever been this match fit in terms of being in front of an audience.'

For a man who never moves his hips, I'm thoroughly enjoying that aspect

It was while playing Frank N.Furter in *The Rocky Horror* show that Jason met stage manager Angela Malloch, now his wife and the mother of his three children Jemma, 11, Zac, 10 and baby Molly. 'The kids have been very supportive,' he says, about his decision to compete. 'But I'm yet to drop them off at the school gates after a week when my scores aren't the best, or if I'm knocked out first! They get to face the public aspect of their dad being on TV on a Saturday night. They're cautiously optimistic but my wife is probably less so!'

Best pal Gary Barlow may be busy on Saturday nights, but he's behind Jason all the way. 'Gary loves *Strictly*, he's a big fan,' reveals Jason. 'I think he quite fancies himself in some sequins and spray tan. But I don't know if he could face losing. He likes to win!'

Len Lightens Up

He has sat in judgement on eight series of *Strictly*, pointing out illegal lifts and getting grumpy over the viewers' votes, but these days Len Goodman is a changed man. Having endured John Sergeant marching through the paso doble, Chris Parker's cape work and the hilarious antics of Ann and Anton, the dance purist is embracing the lighter side of *Strictly*.

'The stunts and rule-breaking used to annoy me more but as I've got older I've mellowed,' he admits. 'I don't know if I'm wrong in changing or should go back to how I was but when I first did *Strictly*, I treated it purely as a dance competition. Then I gradually realised that it is also an entertainment programme and the general public pay their licence fee, switch on and want to be entertained. As much as an old fuddy-duddy like me wants to see "proper" dancing, I think the public like to see things like Hallowe'en week, when the couples dressed up as ghoulies and devils, and I thought it was brilliant.'

Even the bells and whistles of the hi-tech new set, with its video screens and special effects, gets Len's sought-after seal of approval.

'The new set was great,' he comments. 'I thought the whole thing was far more of a production. There was nothing much wrong with the old set but this brightened the whole thing up and made it more sparkly and I really thought they did a great job.'

But for Len, the real icing on the cake of series eight was meeting an idol, who happened to be married to one of the contestants. 'Apart from her dancing, it was great to have Pamela Stephenson there because I got to meet Billy Connolly,' he says. 'I'm a big fan and he was there a lot to support her, so that was great.'

Was Kara the most deserving winner?

Overall, Kara was the best but that came as no surprise. I expected her to be good because young girls like Kara go to ballet and tap and modern dance classes as children, then they go to stage school, and although they're not doing ballroom, they are learning dance. They learn co-ordination and to work their hips, their arms are musical, and that's a huge advantage. Combine that with someone who is in their twenties, pretty good-looking and dancing with a hunky partner – throw in a bit of romance between them, which everybody likes, and you have a potential winner from the off.

Did you predict the other finalists?

When it comes to Matt Baker, I always imagined him as a farmer, traipsing across a muddy field with a pint of cider and a loaf under his arm, on his way to milk the cows! He was a revelation to me. My expectation was that Kara was going to be good. Matt I didn't expect so much and Pamela I didn't expect, but they were incredible.

In the final, Kara and Artem danced the American smooth that broke the rules. Was that a big risk?

There was no proper dancing in that, and they knew I didn't like it, but they knew that everyone else did like it. And I wasn't as a cruel as I was the first time. Craig, Bruno and Alesha loved it in Blackpool. I wasn't keen on Matt's gymnastics either. But you get to a point on the show, in the final, when it becomes a bit of a celebration of the fact that they've got there. The final should be uplifting and positive and to start berating them for this that and the other, I don't think that's the right time to do it. This final was brilliant. Any one of those three could have won and actually it could have been any of the top four, because Scott was great too.

Were you pleased to see a more mature woman in the final?

Pamela was fabulous and James Jordan's routines and choreography were great. It's not about how good the professional is on the dance floor, because you don't want to be distracted by them, so their job is to make the celebrity look great. James did a really good job with a woman who was 60 and maybe not as nimble as some of the younger ones, and she was brilliant.

Who went out too soon?

Goldie didn't deserve to go the first elimination and you could certainly make a case for Paul Daniels or Peter Shilton going out before him. Jimi Mistry was a mystery, because he was kicked out on his best dance, but

'I don't want to be the party pooper but I'm as confused as a baby in a topless bar!'

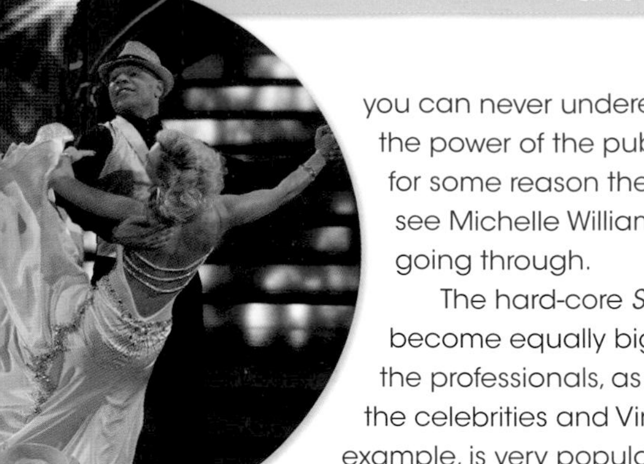

you can never underestimate the power of the public and for some reason they'd rather see Michelle Williams or Ann going through.

The hard-core *Strictly* fans become equally big fans of the professionals, as well as the celebrities and Vincent, for example, is very popular with the public. So as much as they want to see Felicity Kendal, they also want to see Vincent. Brendan has got that edge so, while Michelle Williams wasn't the greatest dancer, they got through.

Who was the biggest disappointment?

A lot of it is to do with your initial expectations and that's why Michelle Williams was such a disappointment. She was in a pop group, used to gyrating, moving about, performing but she was like spiderwoman, all loose limbs. My line for her in one dance was 'Terrible combination. Short skirt, long legs, bad technique.'

Who was the biggest surprise?

Pamela Stephenson, for good reasons, and Ann Widdecombe, because she lasted so long. When I saw her in week 1, I thought, 'She's going home in a minute' but as I said, she was like haemorrhoids – kept coming back more painful than ever.

The *Titanic* routine was fantastic. But as much as you remember really great iconic dances like Chris Hollins' Charleston for good reasons, Ann doing the *Titanic* dance is one you'll never forget, like John Sergeant's paso doble.

Did Ann deserve to stay so long?

Whatever you say about Ann as a dancer, there was always a feeling of anticipation when she was coming out, so I can understand the viewers wanting to see what was going to happen next. Anton did a wonderful job with someone who just couldn't dance at all, which no one else could have done. I don't think she deserved to beat lots of the people she did beat,

but then Gavin only stayed in because he was a hunk. He couldn't dance really. The right four were left in it at the end and I've always said, as long as the best dancers get into the final few, then it doesn't matter what goes on before.

Who did you expect to be bad this time?

That's always the mystery on *Strictly*. Who you expect to be good often isn't and who you think will be terrible might be great. Did anyone expect Pamela Stephenson to end up in the final? You'd never dream of it. And Patsy Kensit, in week 1, was a nervous wreck but gradually her confidence grew and she got better and better. I had a bad feeling about Paul Daniels and that turned out to be correct. I had a feeling that Peter Shilton wouldn't be great, because we had a goalkeeper before, Peter Schmeichel, who was terrible and goalkeepers are used to standing still with their hands out.

How has the series changed over eight series?

The standard has got better and better. I've tried to work out what it is. It could be because the celebrities know now what to expect and go in with a far stronger mindset, and they don't say they'll do it unless they think they have got a chance of doing well. We always get the odd one who is brilliant, like Ricky Whittle, but every year it gets better. I doubt that the series one winner Natasha Kaplinsky would have got much past Patsy Kensit if she was dancing in series eight.

Len's Best Quotes:

After Paul Daniels' rumba
'Parts were magical, parts were comical, parts were diabolical.'

On Ann's quickstep
'Last week you swung to the right but you've got to realise in ballroom you have to lean to the left.'

On Ann's flying tango.
'Watching Ann Widdecombe in a truss coming down from the sky was worth 50 per cent of the TV licence fee.'

On Ann's paso doble
'It was a bit like going up a motorway and there's been an accident on the other side. You don't really want to watch, but you can't help yourself.'

On Kara's American smooth
'I don't want to be the party pooper but I'm as confused as a baby in a topless bar!'

On Gavin's semi-final samba
'You've got the guns but you didn't have the ammunition.'

It's not just the sparkling dresses and dancing shoes that give the *Strictly* girls that touch of glamour. Make-up is a huge part of the dancers' overall look and stylist Lisa Armstrong spends days before each show creating the perfect palate for each dance. On the night of the show, Lisa may have to create two or three looks per female dancer, with only minutes between performances to make the necessary changes. And with HD TV and close up cameras, she can't afford a brush stroke out of place!

Lisa has worked as make-up artist on numerous TV shows before taking over the *Strictly Come Dancing* team in 2008. Who better to share the secrets behind the faces of Latin and ballroom? Here's her step-by-step guide to the *Strictly* look.

Ballroom

The Hollywood Look

Golds and browns for eyes, berry-coloured glossy lips and glowing cheeks

Lisa Armstrong says: 'When you think of the ballroom you think of elegance and sophistication. Choose subtle colours to give a timeless Hollywood feel that will capture the essence of glamour. For the flawless movie star look, choose complementary shades for eyes in soft golds and chocolate browns that work with berry-coloured lip glosses. Always perfect your eye shadow by keeping it understated and well blended. The cheeks can glow with warmth and the lips can shine.'

You will need:

- Three brown eye shadow shades, including a light creamy shade, a mid-brown or rose and a chocolate brown
- A light pink blusher with a hint of shimmer
- A dark berry coloured lip-gloss

Step 1 Sweep a light, creamy shade of eye shadow across the lid and up to the browbone.

Step 2 Pat a mid-brown or rose colour shadow over the lid, fanning out at the outer corner of the eye. Then dab the lighter shade gently in the corner of the eye as a highlighter.

Step 3 Work a dark shade of chocolate brown into the eye socket line and blend into the mid-brown/rose shadow.

Step 4 Use a little of the chocolate shadow underneath the outer corner of the eye to create a stronger look. Make sure you blend everything well.

Step 5 Apply a light shade of blusher to the apple of the cheeks, sweeping outwards with your brush to give a nice shimmery, soft glow.

Step 6 Use a brush to add berry coloured lip-gloss to the middle of the lip and blend outwards to create a fuller lip.

Latin

The Salsa and Samba Look

Colourful and sparkly eyes, natural lip colours

Lisa says: 'Be bold and inspiring, vibrant and as feisty as the excitement of the Samba and Salsa! This is the ultimate feel-good look that will bring colour and sparkle to your everyday life. Choose fun, energetic eye shadows to look hot on the dance floor.'

You will need:

- Three blue eye shadows, including a light shimmery shade, a glittery teal and a strong dark blue
- A blusher in a warm/hot pink
- A lip stain or natural pink lipstick

Step 1 Apply the pale blue eye shadow over the lid, including the corner of the eye, and blend to the outer eye, no higher than the eye socket line.

Step 2 Blend a more vibrant blue or blue-green glittery shadow above the socket line, avoiding the inner corner to produce a strong volume of colour.

Step 3 Use a dark blue around the edge of the eyes, along the upper and lower lash lines.

Step 4 Finish with a touch more of the pale blue below the outer brow as a highlighter.

Step 5 Apply a wash of colour onto the cheeks and over the cheekbones, making sure it's well blended and not too close to the eye line.

Step 6 With the strong eye shadow, only a dab of colour across the lips is needed. Using your finger, dab your lipstick across the lips so that it is almost a lip stain rather than full colour. Keep it fun and vibrant but not too over the top.

The Tango Look

Smoky eyes and timeless ruby red lips

Lisa says: 'This *Strictly* Latin look is a dramatic, energetic expression of style and sensuality. Smouldering charcoals and aubergine eye shadows will give a more intense look whilst ash greys will give the faint hearted a touch of drama paired with timeless red lips.'

You will need:

- Three eye shadows, including a shimmery ash grey shade, a shimmery charcoal grey and a dark purple
- A dark red/brown blusher
- Red lip liner and lipstick

Step 1 Smudge an ash grey shadow on to the eyelids, no higher than the socket line.

Step 2 Use a darker, charcoal grey shadow above the socket line and smooth outwards in a wing like shape.

Step 3 Add a thin line of the charcoal grey along the upper lash line and sweep under the lower lash line. Blend the colours well.

Step 4 Use a dark purple shadow on the outer corners of the upper and lower lash line to intensify the look, adding a little at a time to build up to the dramatic look you want to achieve.

Step 5 To create the structured dramatic look, use a darker blusher underneath your cheekbones, brushing the blusher up your face rather than outwards to give cheeks definition.

Step 6 Before applying the red lipstick use a red lip pencil for the outline, but stick to your lip-line, as going over the lip-line will create a clown-like appearance.

Get help perfecting these looks, devised by expert Lisa Armstrong, and even more fabulous make-up inspiration, with the latest *Strictly* make-up range now available in Boots stores nationwide.

Holly Valance

Like fellow competitor Jason Donovan, Holly Valance went from a lead role in *Neighbours* to an international pop career. But despite her iconic Bollywood-style dancing in the video for her smash hit, *Kiss Kiss,* she reckons she's starting from scratch when it comes to *Strictly.*

'My music videos were me working with a choreographer for two days then shooting it for two days' she says. 'People may think I have something under my belt but I think I probably have less than most – I haven't even done ballet or gymnastics. I did a little bit of jazz when I was eight or nine for a few weeks after school, but that's not really classically trained.'

In fact, she had to discard some of her musical knowledge to get to grips with the steps.

'The rhythm and the pace of what I'm doing now is very different to a musical ear, so I have to throw all that knowledge out the window because this is a whole new kettle of fish,' she explains. 'It doesn't make any difference what I knew before about rhythm. Basically, the usual rules of music don't apply to the cha cha cha, for instance. It has nothing to do with how the music goes and what the beats are, it's not necessarily logical.'

Holly was born in Melbourne to an English mother and Serbian father. At 16, she landed the role of Flick Scully in *Neighbours* and three years later, left the soap to pursue a career in music, topping the charts in 2002 with *Kiss Kiss.* In more recent years she has returned to acting, appearing in *CSI: Miami, Entourage* and *Prison Break* as well as the Liam Neeson movie *Taken.* She now lives in London with her boyfriend, billionaire property tycoon Nick Candy.

The stunning 28-year-old admits to being a little hesitant to take on the *Strictly* challenge but says Nick was keen. 'He told me to take it on and said, "It's a no-brainer,"' she reveals. 'It's a bit out of my comfort zone, and it was something I always thought was cool but I never thought I'd have the courage to do. I was in two minds because the prospect of putting myself out there in front of ten million viewers and competing was quite frightening. But it's such a loved and popular show, and who wouldn't want to be part of something this successful?'

Holly's dance partner is reigning champ Artem Chigvintsev, who lifted the trophy with Kara Tointon in the last series. 'I think that means the expectation is already quite high,' says Holly. 'I'd be happy to have some regular odds against me, not such good odds, because I have to try and live up to them, which is a little bit difficult. But it's making me work harder as well.'

> I was in two minds because the prospect of putting myself out there in front of ten million viewers and competing was quite frightening

And she says the Russian dancer is a joy to work with. 'He's been fantastic, so patient. I can't believe how patient he is with me. He breaks things up so they don't get monotonous. If I'm crumbling, he picks that up. He's very perceptive.'

The Aussie star also has the support of winner Kara, who is now Artem's girlfriend. 'We sort of text each other every couple of days,' she says. 'I have a little whinge and she reassures me. She's been a good source of support.'

Robbie Savage

When Robbie Savage took to the floor for his first dance with Ola Jordan, his fancy footwork was masking his heartbreak over a family tragedy. On that very day, dad Colin, who was diagnosed with a rare form of early Alzheimer's at the age of 56, was going into a residential home.

'I signed up for my mum,' he said. 'It's my mum's favourite show. I'm not looking for a sympathy vote at all but I'm doing it because my father has Alzheimer's and he's only 64. I kept turning it down but my mum said, "Why don't you do it?" and I told her, "For a start I can't dance. I'm not musically minded, I can't count music. It's not for me" But mum said, "You've got to take the opportunity to change people's perceptions of you while you can. Look at your dad."

Robbie was born in Wrexham in 1974 and began his career with Manchester United's Youth Team at 15. He went on to make over 600 appearances for Derby County, Blackburn Rovers, Birmingham City, Leicester City, Crewe Alexandra and Brighton and Hove Albion, as well as playing for the Welsh national team. In recent years he built a successful side-line as a media pundit and in January 2011, he announced his retirement from the sport.

His aggressive style on the pitch has earned the 36-year-old a reputation as one of soccer's hard men and gained him a few enemies among football fans. But Robbie is hoping that his Saturday night stints will change that. 'On the football field I was a winner and I was aggressive, but off the field I'm not like that at all,' he says. 'I'm just a quiet, shy lad, really. Hopefully people's perceptions of me will change.

And while he may have been every referee's nightmare, Robbie is planning to be a pussycat when it comes to the *Strictly* judges.

'I won't be talking back to the judges, because they know more than me. If they played football and I gave them an opinion, I wouldn't expect them to argue with me because I know more about football. They know more about dancing so how on earth can I argue? If they say I'm wrong, I'm wrong.'

Being a six-footer, the blond midfielder was surprised to be teamed with pint-sized professional Ola. 'When we were rehearsing for the group dance nobody thought I'd get Ola,' he reveals. 'It was a shock when they put us together but one of the nicest shocks ever. She's brilliant, she's funny, she's a great teacher. She's like my sister. In fact, we could be brother and sister – we look very similar.'

> On the football field I was a winner and I was aggressive but off the field I'm not like that at all

Robbie, who is married to Sarah and has two boys, Charlie, 8, and Freddie, 4, is giving his all to *Strictly*, training eight hours a day and spending two hours in the gym. But he reckons Ola has her work cut out in the rehearsal room. 'I'm hopeless. I've never danced. I've got a bit of rhythm but I don't dance sober. In fact, I don't dance drunk! I just don't dance.'

TRY SOME STRICTLY STEPS

Strictly Come Dancing has led to a huge uptake in dance classes around the UK but there are still many more potential hoofers holding back. If you have always fancied having a go on the dance floor, but don't know your cucarachas from your kick ball changes, we're here to get you started with a few basic steps extracted from *Strictly Come Dancing: Step-By-Step Dance Class.* So put on your dancing shoes and try a little taste of the Argentine tango, waltz, samba and foxtrot. And when you've mastered those, make sure you 'Keeeeep dancing!'

Argentine Tango

SALIDA
MAN'S STEPS

This figure can be danced in open hold or close embrace.

Start with feet together, weight on left foot
1 Right foot back
2 Left foot side
3 Right foot forward outside partner on lady's right side
4 Left foot forward
5 Right foot closes to left foot
6 Left foot forward
7 Right foot side
8 Left foot closes to right foot
End with feet together, weight on left foot

Notes
Steps 6–8 may turn up to ¼ to left.

When starting with the Salida at the beginning of the dance, it is polite to start with step 2, so the man does not accidentally step backward into another dancer.

SALIDA
LADY'S STEPS

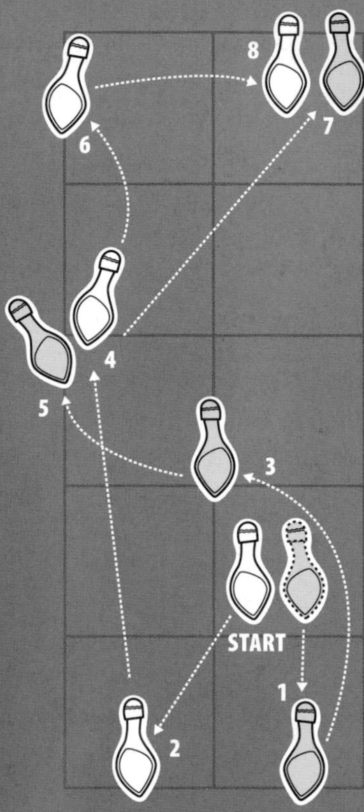

Start with feet together, weight on right foot
1 Left foot forward
2 Right foot side
3 Left foot back
4 Right foot back
5 Left foot crosses in front of right foot ('The Cross')
6 Right foot back
7 Left foot side
8 Right foot closes to left foot
End with feet together, weight on right foot

ROCK STEP AND FORWARD OCHO

MAN'S STEPS

This figure can be danced in open hold or close embrace.

Start with feet together, weight on left foot
1 Right foot back
2 Left foot side
3 Right foot forward outside partner on lady's right side
4 Left foot forward
5 Replace weight back on to right foot
6 Left foot back (small step) just behind right foot – then turn shoulders to the right to lead lady to swivel
7 Right foot closes next to left foot, then turn shoulders to the left to lead lady to swivel, ending in original hold
8–10 Salida steps 6–8
End with feet together, weight on left foot

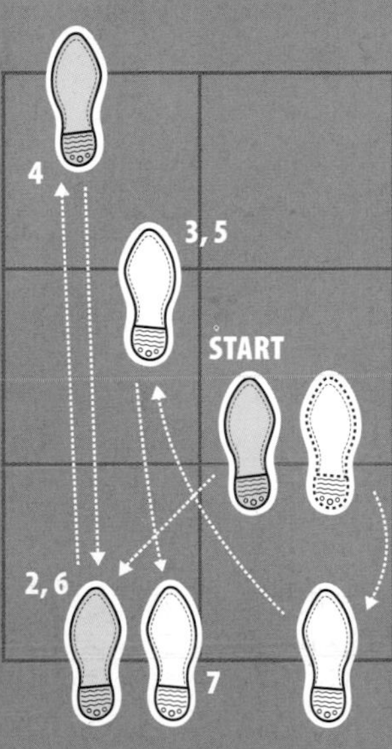

ROCK STEP AND FORWARD OCHO

LADY'S STEPS

Start with feet together, weight on right foot
1 Left foot forward
2 Right foot side
3 Left foot back
4 Right foot back
5 Replace weight forward on to left foot
6 Right foot forward in line with left foot, outside partner on man's right side. When man turns his shoulders, swivel on right foot to the right, ending with left hip closer to man
7 Left foot forward in front of man. When man turns his shoulders, swivel on left foot to the left, ending in original hold
8–10 Salida steps 6–8
End with feet together, weight on right foot

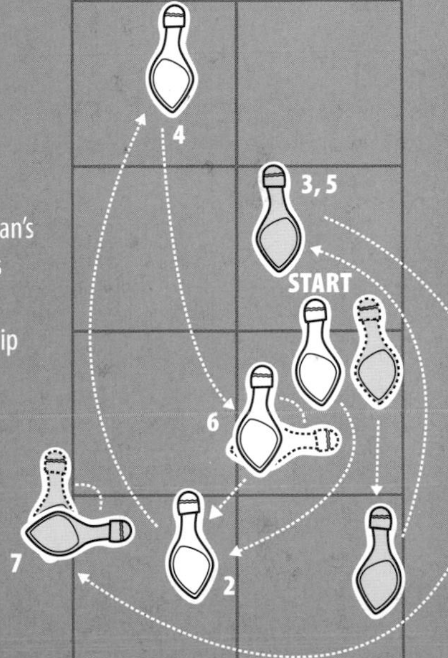

CLOSE EMBRACE

OPEN HOLD

FEATHER STEP
MAN'S STEPS

This figure is danced in closed hold.

Start with weight on left foot
1 Right foot forward (S)
2 Left foot forward (left side leading) (Q)
3 Right foot forward outside partner (Q)
End with weight on right foot
(1. Heel-Toe, 2. Toe, 3. Toe-Heel)

FEATHER STEP
LADY'S STEPS

Start with weight on right foot
1 Left foot back (S)
2 Right foot back (Q)
3 Left foot back (Q)
End with weight on left foot
(1. Toe-Heel, 2. Toe-Heel, 3. Toe-Heel)

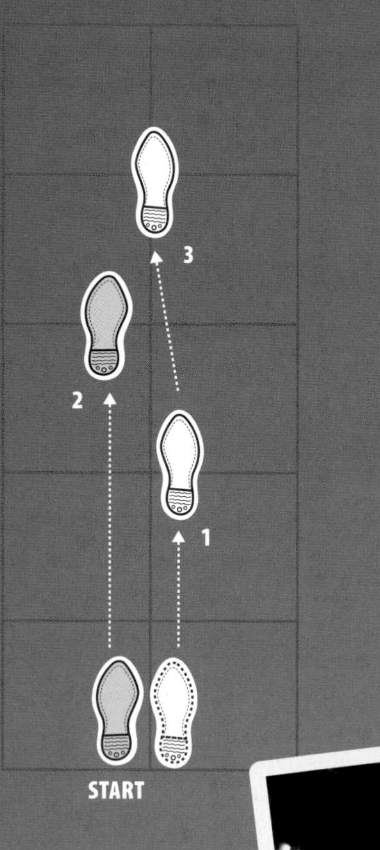

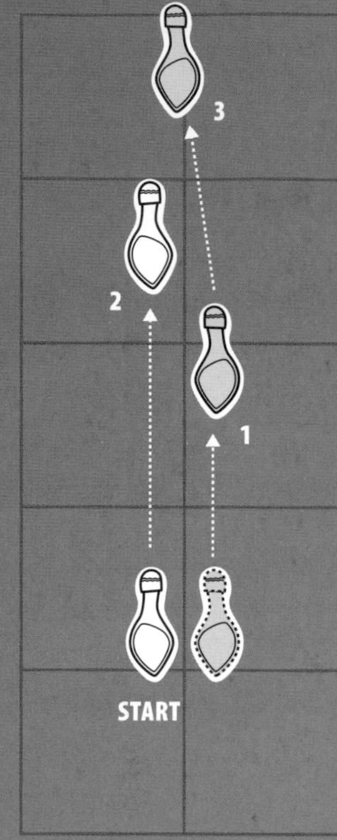

THREE STEP
MAN'S STEPS

This figure is danced in closed hold.

Start with weight forward on right foot outside partner
1 Left foot forward (S)
2 Right foot forward (Q)
3 Left foot forward (Q)
End with weight on left foot
(1. Heel, 2. Heel-Toe, 3. Toe-Heel)

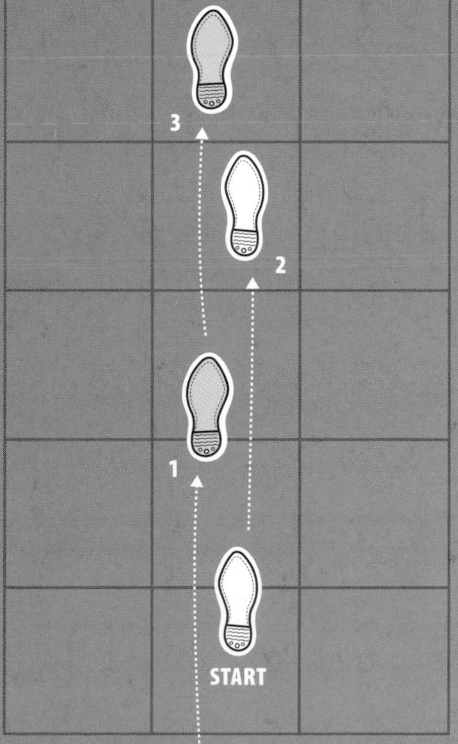

THREE STEP
LADY'S STEPS

Start with weight back on left foot
1 Right foot back (S)
2 Left foot back (Q)
3 Right foot back (Q)
End with weight on right foot
(1. Toe-Heel, 2. Toe-Heel, 3. Toe-Heel)

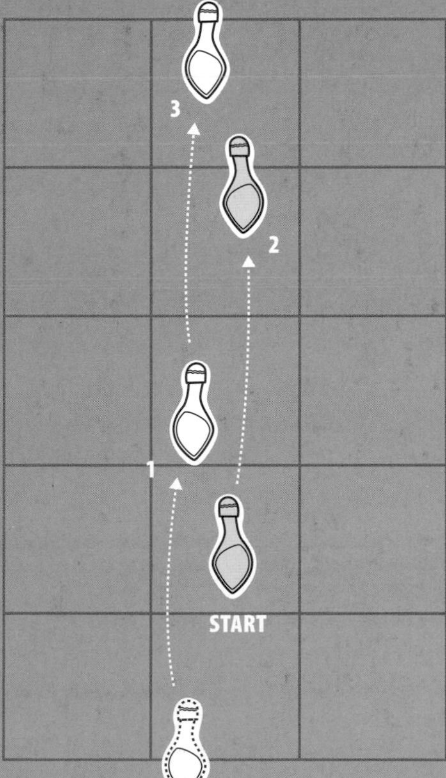

WHISKS
MAN'S STEPS

This figure is danced in closed hold.

Start with weight on right foot
1 Left foot side (1)
2 Right foot crosses behind left foot (a)
3 Replace weight forward on to left foot (2)
4 Right foot side (1)
5 Left foot crosses behind right foot (a)
6 Replace weight forward on to right foot (2)
End with weight on right foot
(1. Ball-Flat, 2. Ball, 3. Ball-Flat, 4. Ball-Flat, 5. Ball, 6. Ball-Flat)

Notes
It is recommended to repeat steps 1–6 before going on to another figure.

To follow Whisks with Samba Walks, man turns ⅛ to left and lady turns ⅛ to right on steps 5–6 to end in promenade position.

WHISKS
LADY'S STEPS

Start with weight on left foot
1 Right foot side (1)
2 Left foot crosses behind right foot (a)
3 Replace weight forward on to right foot (2)
4 Left foot side (1)
5 Right foot crosses behind left foot (a)
6 Replace weight forward on to left foot (2)
End with weight on left foot
(1. Ball-Flat, 2. Ball, 3. Ball-Flat, 4. Ball-Flat, 5. Ball, 6. Ball-Flat)

For all steps with the timing 'a', step on the ball of the foot only, keeping the heel raised.

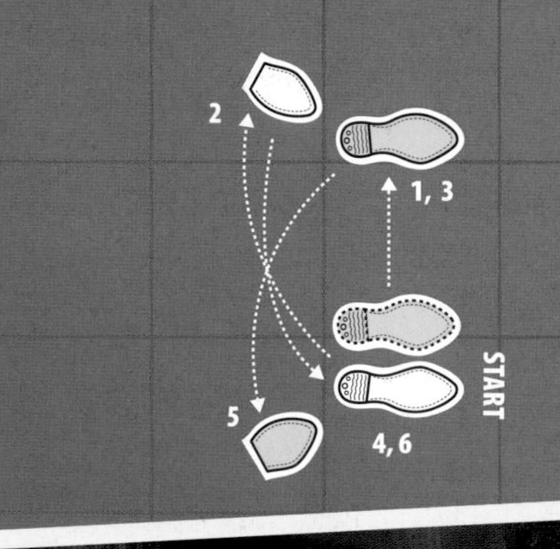

2
1, 3
START
5
4, 6

SAMBA WALKS
MAN'S STEPS

This figure is danced in promenade position.

Start with weight forward on right foot
1 Left foot forward (1)
2 Replace weight back on to right foot (a)
3 Replace weight forward on to left foot (2)
4 Right foot forward (1)
5 Replace weight back on to left foot (a)
6 Replace weight forward on to right foot (2)
End with weight on right foot
(1. Ball-Flat, 2. Ball, 3. Ball-Flat, 4. Ball-Flat, 5. Ball, 6. Ball-Flat)

Note
It is recommended to repeat steps 1–6 before going on to another figure.

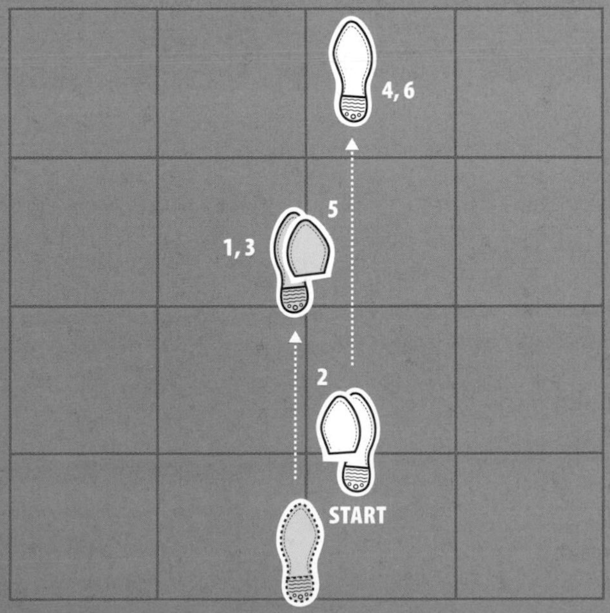

SAMBA WALKS
LADY'S STEPS

Start with weight forward on left foot
1 Right foot forward (1)
2 Replace weight back on to left foot (a)
3 Replace weight forward on to right foot (2)
4 Left foot forward (1)
5 Replace weight back on to right foot (a)
6 Replace weight forward on to left foot (2)
End with weight on left foot
(1. Ball-Flat, 2. Ball, 3. Ball-Flat, 4. Ball-Flat, 5. Ball, 6. Ball-Flat)

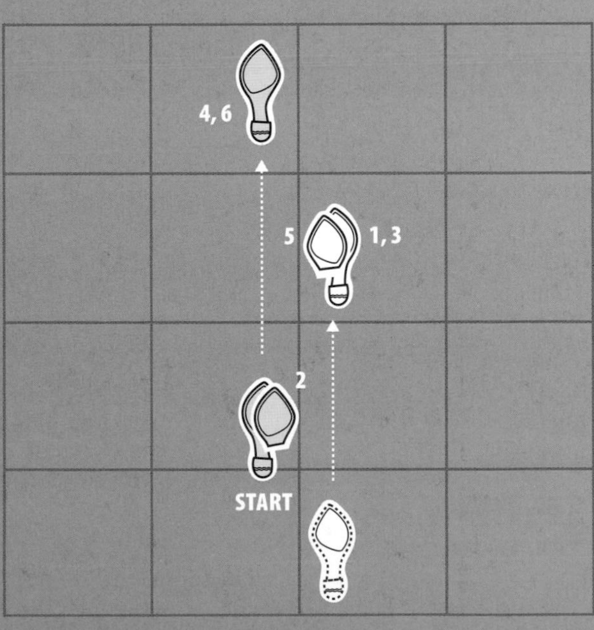

CLOSED CHANGES
MAN'S STEPS

This figure is danced in closed hold.

Start with weight on left foot
1 Right foot forward (1)
2 Left foot side (2)
3 Right foot closes to left foot (3)
4 Left foot forward (1)
5 Right foot side (2)
6 Left foot closes to right foot (3)
End with weight on left foot
(1. Heel-Toe, 2. Toe, 3. Toe-Heel, 4. Heel-Toe, 5. Toe, 6. Toe-Heel)

Note
When dancing Closed Changes only, dance with man moving forward around the floor. When danced in conjunction with other figures, the direction of the Closed Changes will be dictated by the direction of the other figures.

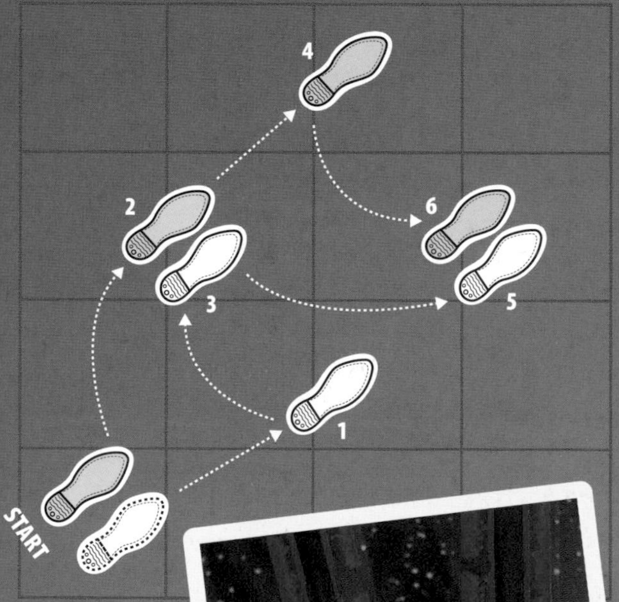

CLOSED CHANGES
LADY'S STEPS

Start with weight on right foot
1 Left foot back (1)
2 Right foot side (2)
3 Left foot closes to right foot (3)
4 Right foot back (1)
5 Left foot side (2)
6 Right foot closes to left foot (3)
End with weight on right foot
(1. Toe-Heel, 2. Toe, 3. Toe-Heel, 4. Toe-Heel, 5. Toe, 6. Toe-Heel)

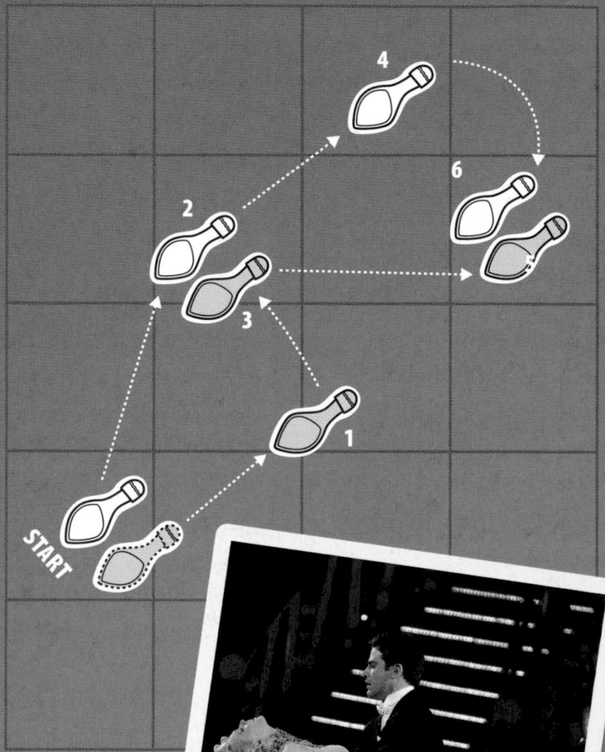

NATURAL TURN
MAN'S STEPS

This figure is danced in closed hold.

Start with weight on left foot
1 Right foot forward (1)
2 Turn ¼ to right, then left foot side (2)
3 Turn ⅛ to right, then right foot closes to left foot (3)
4 Left foot back (1)
5 Turn ⅜ to right, then right foot side (2)
6 Left foot closes to right foot (3)
End with weight on left foot
(1. Heel-Toe, 2. Toe, 3. Toe-Heel, 4. Toe-Heel, 5. Toe, 6. Toe-Heel)

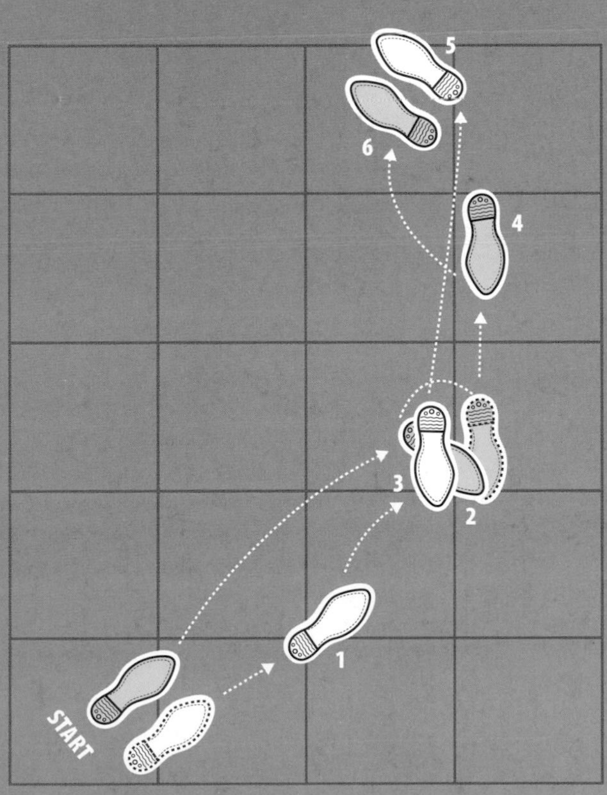

NATURAL TURN
LADY'S STEPS

Start with weight on right foot
1 Left foot back (1)
2 Turn ⅜ to right, then right foot side (2)
3 Left foot closes to right foot (3)
4 Right foot forward (1)
5 Turn ¼ to right, then left foot side (2)
6 Turn ⅛ to right, then right foot closes to left foot (3)
End with weight on right foot
(1. Toe-Heel, 2. Toe, 3. Toe-Heel, 4. Heel-Toe, 5. Toe, 6. Toe-Heel)

The Dancers

Katya Virshilas

The Canadian Kat

After two sportsmen, Katya said her ideal celebrity 'would be in the entertainment business. I've had a cricket player and a rugby player but this year I'm ready for something different.' So she was thrilled to be partnered with *Daybreak* presenter Dan Lobb – even if he is a former tennis player.

The globetrotting hoofer was born in Lithuania and moved to Israel, where she began to study jazz and ballet when she was six. At 13, the family moved to Vancouver, Canada and Katya switched to ballroom and Latin, becoming the youngest-ever British Columbian Latin Dance Champion at the age of 16. In 2000, when she was 17, she was on her travels again, representing Canada at the World Championships in St Petersburg, Russia. After competing and teaching for three more years she was off to Hollywood, to train Richard Gere and Jennifer Lopez for *Shall We Dance*, and landed herself a role in the movie. She went on to dance the tango with Antonio Banderas in *Take the Lead*. She also performed in a stage production for Bollywood choreographer Shiamak Davar, watched by 60,000 spectators.

Katya joined *Strictly* in series 7, dancing with Phil Tuffnell and in the last season, she was charged with coaxing supershy Rugby ace Gavin Henson out of his shell.

'It was amazing and challenging to work with Gavin last season,' she says. 'He was the most scared celebrity and proved everybody wrong. That man CAN dance.'

As well as getting to know Dan, Katya has a new professional partner for series 9, as she has been paired with new boy Pasha. But the relationship will be *Strictly* above board, as the Lithuanian beauty is preparing to walk down the aisle with another dancer, Klaus Kongsdal, next summer.

Ola Jordan

Going for Gold

Former champ Ola Jordan was teamed with Paul Daniels last year, but there was little magic on the dance floor and they were the second couple to leave. It was a stark contrast to the previous year, when she and Chris Hollins waltzed off with the trophy. 'That was unbelievable,' she says. 'I can't describe it. It was a very special day for me especially because I got to the final and I said to my mum and dad that they had to come so they flew from Poland to watch me. It was very special just to be in the final but winning was the cherry on top of the cake.'

Although she often catches husband James staring longingly at the glitterball, she says they back each other all the way. And she was rooting for him in last year's final, when he partnered Pamela Stephenson. 'James was very supportive when I was competing with Chris,' she recalls. 'He wanted me to win. He was nervous for me, but then I was nervous for him when he was in the final this year.'

Ola grew up in Legionowo, near Warsaw, and took up dance classes at the age of 12. In March 2000, James travelled to Poland to try out with her and they instantly hit it off, with Ola moving to the UK to become his partner a month later. Romance blossomed on the dance floor and the pair wed in 2003, before moving to Hong Kong to teach.

Ola, whose skimpy outfits have caused as much of a stir as her fantastic dancing, is looking forward to her sixth *Strictly* season and is keen to score another win with football star Robbie Savage. 'This year I would like to win the trophy again!' she says. 'I am not greedy, but if I didn't want to I wouldn't be doing my job. I want to be the first person to win it twice.'

James Jordan

Dancing Despot

James and wife Ola have recently moved into a new home and the Kent-born hoofer is looking for one last adornment to finish off the décor. Since Ola brought home the glitterball in 2009, James has been desperate to make it a matching pair and last year he came tantalisingly close, finishing third with Pamela Stephenson. 'Last year I got so close to lifting the glitterball trophy, it would be amazing to win it this year,' he says, although he admits he had his doubts when he met partner Pamela, 60.

'When I first got paired with Pamela my initial thought was, oh dear another granny but I didn't realise she was a supergranny!' he laughs. 'She always gave 150 per cent, which got her to the final. I couldn't have been more proud of her.'

Born in Gillingham to former amateur dancers, James began dancing at the age of 11 and met Ola during a trip to Poland ten years later. After four years teaching in Hong Kong, they joined *Strictly* in series four. James insists competing against Ola changes nothing in their everyday relationship. 'We are exactly the same together at work and at home, and I'm not prepared to change my character for anyone,' he says. 'I won't change my attitude just because we are on television and suddenly competing against each other – I'll be the same with my wife on a Saturday night as I will be on a Monday morning.'

James is known for his uncompromising, no-nonsense approach to training, and in the past has reduced his pupils to tears, so he'll be expecting plenty of hard work from celebrity partner Alex Jones.

Aliona Vilani

The Kitten from Kazakhstan

Artem's *Strictly* dance partner was also his rival in the final of series 8. Using celeb partner Matt Baker's talent for gymnastics, her creative routines saw them hit the high notes every week and eventually nab the runner-up spot.

'It was tough but it was a brilliant season and it was fantastic to reach the finals,' she recalls. 'And I have Matt to thank for being such a great friend and for fully trusting me as his teacher and choreographer.'

The talented dancer was relieved at her success with Matt after the previous series when she crashed out of the competition in week 3 with Rav Wilding.

'Matt and I do things in a similar way and have a similar mindset,' she reveals. 'He understood what should be the standard, how to achieve certain things. He was the perfect partner, definitely.'

The stunning redhead grew up in Kazakhstan and began studying classical ballet and performing arts at the age of five. At 11, she switched her attention to ballroom and was soon competing in the finals of the Eastern European competitions. At 13, she was invited to New York to become a member of the Kaiser Dance Academy and she trained in salsa, hip hop and jazz at the prestigious Broadway Dance Center, becoming a US National Champion in Ten Dance at 16. After winning an Amateur Ballroom Championship as part of the US team a year later, she turned professional. In 2006, Aliona moved to LA and two years later she competed in *Dancing with the Stars*. This year will be her third season on *Strictly* and she's looking forward to teaching Harry Judd how to dance to the beat.

'There is nothing more satisfying and rewarding than taking an untrained artist and watching them blossom. My hope for Harry this year is nice and simple: if he'll give me his best efforts I promise to do my best to make the dancing fun, exciting and great!'

Artem Chigvintsev

From Russia with Love

Latin expert Artem certainly knows how to make an entrance. As one of the new boys in series eight he managed to steal the *Strictly* crown *and* get the girl, beautiful champ Kara Tointon. The couple are still very much an item, a year after they danced to victory together.

'She is the kindest and the most talented person I know and working with her on *Strictly* was magical,' says the romantic Russian.

Artem was born and raised in Izhevsk, Russia, and began dancing at a young age after his mother enrolled him in classes, keen to find a hobby that would keep him out of trouble.

When he began to win competitions he decided to pursue it as a career and at 15 he moved to Germany to train. After further coaching in England and Italy he moved to Los Angeles, where he has choreographed for the show *So You Think You Can Dance* as well as taking a few acting roles, including a part in *The O.C.* Most recently Artem performed as part of a major dance show on a worldwide tour. The same tour gave him the opportunity to perform on Broadway as well as on the West End stage.

It will be hard for the hunky hoofer to top the triumph of last year's *Strictly*, although he and Aussie singer Holly Valance are hot favourites. But Artem says he will be happy as long as she 'has a passion for dance and wants to have the time of her life! The most important thing is to find out what she's good at, find her individual talents and make the most of them.'

Robin Windsor

British Beefcake

Muscle-bound Robin's skimpy tops made quite an impression on the ladies when he made his debut in series 8, and there's plenty more to come. 'I have already purchased a brand-new set of vests!' he laughs. But he proved he was more than just a pretty face by helping Patsy Kensit find her own confidence after a very shaky start. 'It was an honour to have Patsy as my first celebrity,' he says. 'Week 1 was a dis-ah-ster but she grew and grew and left the show a beautiful confident ballroom dancer – a very special lady and a friend for life.'

He's looking forward to having a similar effect on new partner Anita Dobson. 'This year I'm up for the challenge. Whether she is the next Ann Widdecombe or the next Kara Tointon, I'm ready. Bring it on!

Robin grew up near Ipswich and was dancing by the time he was three. 'I was born to dance,' he says. At 15 he moved to London to pursue his career, but retired from competitive dancing at 20 before touring in a dance show which travelled the world and even took him to the Broadway stage.

The beefy ballroom dancer is a romantic at heart and loves the waltz. But he also likes to notch up the energy on the dance floor. 'I love all high energy, fast dances where you can really go for it,' he says. 'The jive is such a crowd pleaser.'

And as if he doesn't get enough exercise in the training room, Robin loves to spend his spare time working out in the gym. 'It's a great place to relieve any stress,' he says. 'I don't get angry – I just take out my tension at the gym!'

Kristina Rihanoff

Blonde Bombshell

Russian minx Kristina is yet to find a partner who she can get to the final. In the three series she's taken part in so far, the closest she has got was with John Sergeant! He was the first celeb contestant she was paired with and, despite the public backing him week after week, he left the competition in week 9.

'I didn't know what to expect for my first year on the series,' she says. 'It was the biggest surprise of my professional career to be partnered by John Sergeant. When I saw him I thought 'Oh my God, what am I going to do? But I learnt the show is not only about dancing but also winning over the audience at home.'

The following year she was teamed with boxer Joe Calzaghe, who made up for his lack of dancing ability by sweeping her off her feet, and they are still a couple. But series 8 proved the most disappointing yet, when Kristina and Goldie were voted out in week 1.

'Goldie was probably the most surprising partner I've ever had,' she says. 'It was a shock to leave in the first week, and was the saddest experience, as I really wanted us to go further.'

The sexy Siberian, who has been dancing since she was six, visited London as a small child and is thrilled to be back in Britain. 'The UK is a very special country for me,' she says. 'When I was a little girl I came here hoping to achieve my dreams in my dance career. Once again, my life has brought me to London and given me an amazing opportunity to follow my dreams!'

This year's partner, Australian singer Jason Donovan, may be her best hope yet and he can expect hard work but also a lot of fun in the training room. 'I have been teaching a lot of beginners and you need to find a way to make it simple for them while having fun and finding cool ways to explain things. Then, even when the work gets hard, they still feel like they are having a good time and accomplishing great things.

Brendan Cole

Hot-headed Hoofer

Series 8 partner Michelle Williams brought out the sensitive side of fiery professional Brendan Cole. As well as defending her against the judges, he turned counsellor in the training room, handing out hugs, tissues and pep talks. 'Michelle expects so much from herself,' he said during one tough week. 'She is trying to run before she can walk and I get the feeling that this week she's a little scared. It's a horrible thing to watch someone breaking in front of your very eyes.' He even arranged a secret visit from best pal and former Destiny's Child bandmate, Kelly Rowland.

'Brendan is great,' said his grateful partner. 'He really looks after me. I get really down when I don't remember the steps, but Brendan is always there to make me laugh. He doesn't let me stay down.'

Sadly, Brendan's father passed away during the last series and he was forced to miss a week, but on the whole he enjoyed series 8. 'We had an amazing time dancing together and she always had so much energy in the training room, which is what you want from your partner,' he says.

Brendan was born in Christchurch, New Zealand and began dance classes, reluctantly, at the age of six. He soon realised his love for dance and was competing at seven. Along with younger sister Vanessa, the Cole children soon made a name for themselves and at one point all three were in the top five of New Zealand dancers. At 18, he moved to the UK. Brendan's greatest triumph on the show was winning series 1 with Natasha Kaplinsky and he's keen to do it again with this year's partner, Lulu. 'I would love to lift the trophy this year,' says the ambitious professional. 'So I hope Lulu will prove as competitive as I am!'

Natalie Lowe

Hot to Trot

Natalie Lowe is one lucky lady. In the two series she has been competing in *Strictly Come Dancing*, she has landed two of the hottest and most talented male celebs the show has ever seen. Her first *Strictly* partner, Ricky Whittle, turned out to be a sensational dancer but was pipped at the post by Chris Hollins. And last year, *EastEnders* star Scott Maslen mastered the Latin moves and the elegance of the ballroom.

'I was extremely lucky to have been given the opportunity to dance with Scott last series; he had a very special quality about his dancing that is very hard to find in the celebrity dancers. His passion to learn and his unique, energetic, charismatic personality left me feeling like he captured the passion of dance, I felt like we embraced the *Strictly* experience to the fullest.'

Natalie was born in Sydney, Australia and watched her older siblings, Glenn and Kylie, dance until she was old enough to join in. 'I grew up with only one thing on my mind: ballroom dancing,' she says. 'I enjoyed music and athletics at school but dancing became my sole purpose in life!'

Partnered with brother Glenn, she joined adult competitions at an early age, they won several national titles and decided to move overseas to further their dance careers. When a family illness thwarted their plans, however, fate took a turn and Natalie was asked to be a professional on *Dancing with the Stars* in Australia. During her seven years, she reached the final six times and won once. The Aussie champ, who is dancing with boxer Audley Harrison, is a firm believer in a balance of hard work and playfulness in the training room. 'Patience is the key, keep it fun, but know that it has to be quality rehearsal time.'

Flavia Cacace

Queen of the Soaps

It could be because of her bubbly personality but in four out her five series, Flavia has found herself partnering a former soap star. In series 5 she reached the final with *EastEnders* star Matt di Angelo, making it all the way to the final and finishing second behind Alesha Dixon. The soap bubble burst the following year when Matt's co-star Phil Daniels only managed one dance, and in series 7, Craig Kelly failed to win the judges' votes, despite making in to Blackpool.

Last year EastEnder-turned-film-star Jimi Mistry brought a touch of Tinseltown to the dance floor, but competition was fierce and the couple left in week 6. 'What can I say about Jimi?' laughs Flavia. 'Charming, funny, hard-working and a great mover!!"

Born in Italy, Flavia moved to Guildford at the age of four and met partner Vincent Simone at a local dance school when she was 17. The couple went on to become champions in Ten Dance and their speciality, the Argentine tango and have now danced together for 13 years. Since last year's *Strictly* they have toured the country with their show *Midnight Tango*, playing 130 dates, and will transfer to the West End in January 2012. '*Midnight Tango* has been the biggest and most proud achievement of my career,' she says.

For this series, Flavia will be seeing stars in more ways than one, having been teamed with astronomer Russell Grant. Although she will expect him to be 'enthusiastic and willing to win', Flavia prides herself on her patience in the training room and says, 'I like to use examples when I'm teaching as I think that helps people to understand what I'm trying to say.'

Vincent Simone

Italian Stallion

In 2008, tango king Vincent Simone came within a whisker of winning the trophy with Rachel Stevens, losing out on the final showdance to Tom Chambers and Camilla Dallerup. This season he is hoping Edwina Curry's political spin will take him to the final.

'I hope Edwina will be excited to be part of this amazing show and very keen on winning,' he says. 'I think this is my year to win and lift the glitterball trophy."

Series 8 saw the pint-sized romeo living *The Good Life* with Felicity Kendal, who proved incredibly supple despite being a granny in her sixties. And the pair got on like a house on fire. 'Felicity was a true star,' he recalls. 'I loved every minute working with her, she loved me and the show so much, and the chemistry we had together made us a success.'

Vincent was born and raised in Foggia, near Naples, and joined a dance school when he was seven, along with his parents, who are now ballroom and Latin teachers. 'It was a real family affair – we all started learning to dance together and we loved it.' After becoming Italian Juvenile Champion for four years running, he decided to move to the UK at 16, and soon teamed up with fellow Italian Flavia.

The couple joined the *Strictly* team in series 4, when Vincent reached the quarter-finals with soap star Louisa Lytton. 'My first time on *Strictly*, I was extremely lucky to be paired up with Louisa as she was probably one of the most talented celebrities ever to have taken part,' he says.

This year Edwina can expect hard work, passion and plenty of flirting from her Italian tutor but, he insists, they will be the best of friends.

Erin Boag

Strictly's Miss Whiplash

Like dance partner Anton, Erin Boag has competed in all eight series of *Strictly* and is looking forward to the ninth. But after two rugby players, two goalkeepers, a snooker player and an Olympic athlete, she is ready for a change. So she's delighted to be paired with impressionist Rory Bremner.

Even so, her greatest success on the show came with Colin Jackson, who danced his way into the final, only to be pipped at the post by Darren Gough. 'Colin was an absolute star and I believe one of the best male celebrities to ever appear on *Strictly Come Dancing*,' says the Kiwi.

But the most emotional exit for the nimble New Zealander came in series six, after she was eliminated from the quarter-finals with beefcake Austin Healey.

'I have never laughed so much in my life as I did with Austin,' she recalls. 'We had the best time but both of us were so upset when we got knocked out so close to the end.'

Last year she and former England goalkeeper Peter Shilton failed to make it past the third round, but she still insists, 'it was such a pleasure and honour to dance with a great legend.'

Born in Auckland, Erin is the daughter of two professional dancers who literally fell in love on the dance floor. Beginning with ballet lessons at three, Erin adored dancing and at 18, she became the New Zealand Ten-Dance Amateur Champion. After moving to Australia, then the UK, she took four separate jobs, working as a nanny as well as ironing, cleaning and dress-making, to support herself through dancing and living in London. In 1997, she met dance partner Anton Du Beke.

Dubbed Miss Whiplash by Colin Jackson, Erin can be a tough teacher and Rory will need to pay attention. 'I can work with most people,' she says. 'If they are willing to learn and have good concentration then I am happy.'

Anton Du Beke

Joker in the Pack

Ballroom specialist Anton Du Beke found his legendary sense of humour extremely useful in series 8. Paired with the formidable Ann Widdecombe, he had his work cut out in the training room and at one point he joked, 'It's like being in control of a runaway train.' But the creative choreographer's inventive routines turned bad dancing into hilarious performances and kept the public on side all the way to the quarter-finals, despite the judges' low scores.

'Ann was brilliant to work with,' recalls Anton. 'And I've got countless highlights from last year!'

Born and raised in Sevenoaks, Kent, Anton was a relative latecomer to ballroom dancing, joining a local class at the age of 14. A football fanatic before then, he was dragged into the dancehall by his sister's teacher, and soon discovered it was a great place to meet girls.

At 17, he decided to specialise in ballroom and after leaving school he landed a job as a baker to pay his way on the dance circuit. He would get up at 3am, work all day and practise all evening.

When he's not on the dance floor Anton is likely to be found on the golf course, where he has been known to tee off with Bruce Forsyth, one of his great heroes.

Anton is one of only three dancers from *Strictly*'s first series who is still competing, along with Erin and Brendan Cole. He is yet to get his hands on the trophy, but has taught celebs of all abilities, from the elegant actress Laila Rouass and singer Lesley Garrett, who finished third in series 1, to the more challenging Ann Widdecombe and Kate Garraway. This year, he is paired with another formidable lady in Italian lawyer Nancy Dell'Olio and he's hoping she'll be an enthusiastic pupil. 'I don't have an ideal celebrity partner,' he says. 'I just want someone who will love the experience and the challenge!'

Pasha Kovalev

A Russian Revolution

Pasha Kovalev may come from the frozen lands of Siberia but he's bound to melt a few hearts when he takes to the dance floor. *Strictly*'s new boy has muscles to rival Artem's and a sense of humour which helped him slot into the team with ease.

'I was very excited about meeting the other dancers,' he says. 'They are really cool guys. They know how to take a joke. At the beginning, I was sussing out normal things, like how to react to James's jokes! But I felt really welcome because everyone was trying to help me with everything.'

The Russian was particularly happy to be paired with Katya for the professional dances, as they get on like a house on fire. 'I think we clicked straight away,' he recalls. 'Sometimes people cannot really work together, but I think we are perfectly fine and I hope she's enjoying dancing with me too.'

Pasha is the first dancer in his family, having fallen in love with ballroom at a local competition that his mum took him to when he was eight. 'I was really impressed with the show and immediately asked my mum to take me to the local dance studio and that's how it all started,' he says. And he believes that Russia is a perfect place for a budding dancer to grow up 'It is as prestigious to be a dancer as to be a football player,' he explains. 'Maybe that's why Russia is very famous for raising great dancers known around the whole world.'

After many years of training in his homeland, Pasha moved to Los Angeles where he appeared as a finalist in the third season of *So You Think You Can Dance*. He went on to tour in the stage show *Burn the Floor*, before signing up for this year's *Strictly*. And his new job meant a move from L.A. to London. 'Both of these things are a dream come true,' he says enthusiastically. '*Strictly* is an amazing show to be part of and I've wanted to be on it for quite some time. And London is a city I've always dreamed of living in. So I guess it's a good thing they come together as a package.

'I now live near Hyde Park, and I love just walking around. I try not to take a taxi, tube or bus because I prefer to walk. Being in London is like being in a museum. Everywhere you go is steeped in history and I love that.'

Even though it's his first series, he has high hopes for his celebrity partner, *Waterloo Road* star Chelsee Healey.

'I was thrilled to get Chelsee because in the first few rehearsals they had for the group dance, I saw that she really can move,' he reveals. 'She has rhythm, she feels the music and, of course, some proper training is required, but I think she could be very, very good. It's hard for me to say whether we can win because at this point I have no idea what the other celebrities will look like and what their partnerships will be like.'

Unlike some of her competitors, Chelsee is still working full-time, filming the next series of *Waterloo Road* while training, which means a lengthy commute for Pasha. 'I'm going to be going back and forth between London and Manchester because we'll need to grab as much time as we can and it's going to be really tough for her,' he says. 'But she's very excited that she's doing *Strictly* so she's ready to do some real damage.'

A ballroom and Latin all-rounder, who has vast teaching experience, is still deciding whether to bring the carrot or the stick to the training sessions.

'Teaching is like psychology in a lot of ways' he explains. 'You have to find the proper approach to fit the personality, the way they take in information, how hard you can push them, when you have to be sweet and nice and when you have to crack the whip, so with every person, I'm different.'

Before meeting her partner on the launch show, cheeky Chelsee joked that as a single girl she was hoping for some 'eye-candy'. The sexy Siberian could be the answer to her prayers and *Strictly*'s newest recruit hasn't ruled out a romance.

'She said it for a joke,' he insists. 'But she's a lovely girl and I only met her a couple of times for a few brief moments, so we'll see how we get on. Not that I'm looking for a relationship! At the moment, I don't even know what kind of personality she has. From the first look, she's very bubbly and very out there but once we get to work it could be a completely different picture!'

Strictly QUIZ

Are you a jiving genius or a dancing dunce? When it comes to *Strictly* are you the Paul Daniels of ballroom or a budding Kara Tointon. Find out how much you know about your favourite show with the first round of our quiz, and see if you can make it through the dance off to play in the second.

1 Which judge often vows, 'I'll pickle me walnuts'?

2 Which former boyband member performed his hit 'Rock DJ' on the first results show of series 8?

3 To which track did Chris Hollins and Ola Jordan perform their winning Charleston in the series 7 final?

4 Name the first couple to lift the coveted trophy in series 1?

5 How many couples competed in series 1?

6 Which funnyman advised his competing celebrity wife with the following rhyme? 'There's only one way to succeed at the rumba. Keep your back straight and wiggle your bumba.'

7 Which two judges took part in the 2010 Children in Need special, when pop stars Harry Judd and Rochelle Wiseman were the contestants?

8 Which TV presenter partnered Brendan Cole in series 3?

9 Which year did current judge Alesha Dixon win the trophy?

10 In which dance would Len be looking for clean, sharp 'kicks and flicks'?

11 Which two professional dancers are husband and wife?

12 Which rugby player was beaten to the glitterball by Mark Ramprakash in series 4?

13 What caused Jade Johnson to pull out of series 7 early?

14 Which dance would a man be doing if he was holding a cape?

15 Which professional dancer announced she would retire from the show after winning with actor Tom Chambers?

The First Dance

DANCE OFF QUESTION.

Name four Latin dances regularly danced by individual couples in *Strictly Come Dancing.*

Now calculate your score using the answers at the back of the book and work out your position on the judges' leader board.

Under 5

Craig says, 'You are a dance disaaaaster, darling.' Bottom of the leader board. Your only hope is the public vote. Go to the dance off question to see the phone lines can save you.

Between 5 and 10

Len says, 'It's good but it's not great. You're up against some stiff competition and you've got to up your game. If you can nail the next round, you could be a contender.'

You're in the dance off. Answer the question to go through.

Over 10

Bruno says, 'You ballroom beauty. A stunning performance.' You're straight through to the next round.

Answers 1. Len Goodman 2. Robbie Williams 3. 'Fat Sam's Grand Slam' 4. Natasha Kaplinsky and Brendan Cole 5. Eight. 6. Billy Connolly 7. Craig Revel Horwood and Len Goodman 8. Fiona Phillips 9. 2007 10. The jive 11. James and Ola Jordan 12. Matt Dawson 13. A knee injury 14. Paso Doble 15. Camilla Dallerup. Dance off question possible answers: paso doble, samba , salsa, rumba, cha cha cha, jive

Lulu

Singer and songwriter Lulu amazed audiences when she performed a streetdance to Soulja Boy's 'Crank That' for the 2011 *Let's Dance for Comic Relief.* The experience persuaded her to sign up for this year's *Strictly.*

'Comic Relief lulled me into a false sense of security,' she laughs. 'I had so much fun and it was hard, but I like hard work. I like to learn. I like to challenge myself and that's what made me think that I could possibly do it.'

But she admits that she may not live up to everybody's expectations on the *Strictly* dance floor. 'Everyone says, "You'll be great. You'll be fine" and I may not be great or fine. I'm not a trained dancer and I'm finding it very, very hard to count the way dancers count. Basically, I'm intuitive and dancing comes instinctively to me, but this is something people have been trained for. So I feel like a baby taking baby steps, and sometimes it's scary because I think, are you kidding yourself?'

And she reveals that she warned Brendan he was in for a bumpy ride. 'When I watched the launch show, I texted Brendan and said, "Oh baby, you have got your work cut out! There ain't nothing fluid about my movements." Everything is jerky with me,' she says. 'He got back and said, "Yeah, I know."'

Lulu was born Marie MacDonald McLaughlin Lawrie in Lennoxtown, Glasgow, and became a star at 15, when her raucous rock anthem *Shout* shot into the top ten. In 1966, she starred in *To Sir With Love* and sang the title song, a huge hit in the US, and two years later she won the *Eurovision Song Contest* with *Boom Bang-a-Bang.* In 1993, she was back in the limelight when she sang on Take That's hit, *Relight My Fire* and in 2004 she released *Together,* an album of duets with such stars as Sting, Paul McCartney and Elton John.

The bubbly singer admits she was shocked when she drew Brendan as a dance partner, because of his reputation as a hothead.

'In the short time before we found out who our partners were, everyone talked about him being the bad boy, hot-tempered, and I thought, blimey, I don't want that,' she recalls. 'So I was shocked beyond belief because I wanted a patient soul, but so far he has the patience of a saint.

> I like to challenge myself and that's what made me think that I could possibly do it

'Brendan is an amazing teacher. He just keeps hammering home what he thinks I need to know in order to help me. I think we're still in the honeymoon period, although he shouted at me yesterday, and quite rightly. I was shocked but I think he was trying to shake me into focussing when he felt I had lost my focus.'

The 62-year-old star says everyone around her has *Strictly* fever, but she is too anxious to catch it just yet.

'My nieces and my daughter-in-law are more excited about everything than I am,' she reveals. 'People are beyond excited! It's like the country has *Strictly* fever. But I can't see the wood for the trees. With me it's all about the shoes hurting my feet, I can't get that step, my knees don't straighten and I can't count the beats. I've got the two sides of the coin. There's a scared little girl inside as well as that, 'bring it on!' attitude.'

Rory Bremner

After years of entertaining the nation with his brilliant impersonations, Rory Bremner is hoping to make a good impression on the judges and the viewers with his fancy footwork. But will he be appearing as himself or will he take on the mantle of a famous dancer to get through?

'I have had my friends saying "Can you do the paso doble as Des Lynam?" And I'm weighing up whether to do the salsa as William Hague,' he jokes. 'Somebody did suggest that I should try to imitate one of the great Hollywood stars which is fine, but the one I'm imitating at the moment is Shrek!'

Rory was born in Edinburgh and studied modern languages at King's College, London. He first sprung to fame with his parody of Paul Hardcastle's '19', imitating cricket commentators on the track 'N-N-Nineteen Not Out' in 1985. By 1987, he had his own BBC show, *Now - Something Else* and six years later he moved to Channel 4 with *Rory Bremner, Who Else?* Along with John Bird and John Fortune, he hosted *Bremner, Bird and Fortune* from 1999 to 2010, gaining several Bafta nominations and the 2003 Broadcasting Press Guild Award.

Dance partner Erin Boag is getting the benefit of his award-winning talents in training. 'I'm trying to keep the impressions at bay but I tend to do them when I'm nervous or just when I'm in a good mood. I do impressions like people sing. So yesterday Erin had four different dance partners. She danced with Julian Clary – who she's danced with before, so she got a litte bit of déjà vu – then Vince Cable, who she's also danced with before. Then we got into an argument about 'mansion tax' so Gordon Brown came into the equation and finally she got Nelson Mandela because she told me I was dancing like an old man!'

Erin has been having so much fun it seems she is failing to live up to her nickname of Miss Whiplash. 'Erin is a dream. She's lovely to work with. She hasn't had to crack the whip yet because I'm there,' reveals Rory. 'I find it easier to capitulate. I came into this with my hands up.'

But the 50-year-old comedian, who now lives in Oxfordshire, is hard enough on himself. 'I'm a little bit of a perfectionist,' he says. 'If I'm doing something, I like to do it really well and the key to me is that I am a chameleon – I've already changed colour with the fake tan. But I always try to adapt to the environment and that does mean putting in the hours and trying to get it right.'

I'm trying to keep the impressions at bay but I tend to do them when I'm nervous or just when I'm in a good mood

And Rory, who is away from wife Tessa and his two girls Ava, 9,and Lila, 7, while training in London, is becoming a changed man. 'I lost half a stone in the first week,' he said. 'I think it's a combination of eating more healthily and exercise. And Robbie Savage has been telling me about ice baths and stuff like that, so in the hotel I get buckets of ice and chuck it in the bath and sit in that for five or ten minutes. It's good for the muscles and it's actually surprisingly good fun.'

Political Spin

After 23 years in the House of Commons, politician Ann Widdecombe found an altogether new way to cross the floor when she took on the *Strictly* challenge. As she walked down the steps on the launch show, the audience were already behind her and, asked what he was most looking forward to in season eight Craig replied, 'Two words. Ann Widdecombe.'

Unlike most politicians, the former minister lived up to her promise. After her week 1 waltz with partner Anton Du Beke, she joked 'If you think that's bad, you should see the salsa.' And she wasn't wrong. Indeed, the week 2 performance left Craig almost speechless. 'There is not one word in the English language which can describe what over ten million people have just witnessed,' he spluttered, while Bruno told her, 'It was unique and compelling, somewhere between horror and comedy. An out-of-body experience that kind of resembled a dance.'

From then on Ann was bottom of the leader board in seven of the ten weeks on the show. She broke three records for the lowest scores on specific dances and matched two more. But while her clod-hopping performances failed to impress the judges, the viewers were exercising their right to vote, and gave her a clear majority. The judges, who have been known to speak out against similar situations in the past, greeted Ann's success with calm acceptance.

'It was different than it was with John Sergeant,' explains Craig, 'because we knew he was capable of doing better and then we see him stomping around through laziness. But Ann has always said, and will always continue to say, that she can't dance, and I know that to be completely and utterly true after dancing with her on the tour. She can't retain anything, she can't hear the music, and she's the first to admit that.'

Ann's secret weapon was laughter. With inventive routines and great use of props, Anton's flair for comedy was unleashed and each week the hilarious couple left the viewers wanting more.

'Anton is very funny,' says Ann. 'Even though we were doing comedy, the show was nevertheless competitive so we had to come up with comedy good enough to let us survive each week, and something different each week. Anton was wonderful at that.'

With each week came a new gimmick. In week 6, Ann kissed a portrait of Craig at the end of the Charleston and the week 9 rumba, to the *Titanic* theme tune 'My Heart Will Go On', came with a ship's bell, fake fog and a whopping great iceberg. Sadly,

No.
Scene 2
Take
Date
Sound
Prod. Co.
Director
Cameraman

that handed ammunition to Aussie judge Craig, who told Ann, 'That iceberg showed more emotion.'

But the *pièce de résistance* was the couple's week 4 tango, which saw the formidable lady sailing down to the dance floor on a flying rig. An amused Len laughed, 'Watching Ann Widdecombe in a truss coming down from the sky was worth 50% of the TV licence fee.' Bruno commented, 'Truly out of this world. Was it a bird? Was it a plane? No, it's Starship Widdecombe,' and Craig added, 'I thought it was more like the Dancing Hippos, darling. At the beginning it was gorgeous, ethereal, it was light, beautiful, and then you landed on the floor and that's when the problems began.' But the stunt captured the imagination of the nation and even made it into Prime Minister David Cameron's speech at the CBI the following week. 'Like Ann Widdecombe, I had to be hitched by a wire over the audience to get to the stage,' he told the gathered business leaders as he arrived.

Shrewd operator Ann knew it was the public who she needed on side if she wanted to stay. 'I'm not trying to impress the judges,' she said at the time. 'The judges wouldn't be impressed if I did a virtuoso *Swan Lake*, so forget the judges.'

In week 10, however, the mood changed on the judging panel and, after an American smooth which proved pretty rough, Alesha told her, 'I can't see any improvement and I'm sorry but for me the honeymoon is over!' Len added to the call to put an end to her run when he added, 'I don't want to be nasty, because you've given me fun, but snow gives you fun to start with and eventually you just want it to go away.' Sadly, the viewers agreed and the comedy couple had had their last laugh.

'It's clear to me that the public have finally come to their senses,' said Craig. 'And I do trust the great British public that they will choose the best dancer in the end.'

'It had to come sometime,' said a philosophical Ann, 'but it's been great fun so thank you viewers for keeping me in when those four icebergs would have got rid of me.'

For the retired MP, who was looking forward to learning three dances for the semi-finals, it was a disappointment but not a surprise.

'I was a bit disappointed that we didn't last one more week,' she says. 'I thought we had one more week in us. That may have made us a bit complacent, actually, but I never expected to get to the final because as the cookie crumbled, we were up against four very good dancers. If we'd had two very good dancers, we might have squeezed in but there were four and so to get to the final I would have had to knock out not one but two, and that would have been ridiculous. It wasn't going to happen and it shouldn't happen.'

The elimination meant the public never got to see her final showdance, which may have seen more aerial antics. She teased, 'If Anton had his way, we were going to fly in from separate directions and do some dancing in the air, underneath the glitterball.'

But the *Strictly* experience didn't end there for the Conservative stalwart. She went on to dance with nemesis Craig Revel Horwood on tour and brought the house down every night. And she will be reunited with him at Christmas, when they star in a pantomime together. In the meantime, Ann has returned to her second career as an author but she is delighted she had the chance to appear in the show.

'To say I'm glad is an understatement,' she says. 'It was wonderful, it was life-enhancing, I'm just very sorry that it came to an end. I've made some friends but the main thing is that I've enjoyed the whole business of performing and making people laugh.'

So will she be tripping the light fantastic on a regular basis now? 'Don't be silly,' she insists, with characteristic frankness. 'I didn't learn to dance in the entire programme. Apart from the odd charity function I don't expect I'll ever dance again.'

Nancy Dell'Olio

As well known for her outrageous dress sense as her high profile love life, Nancy Dell'Olio is bound to cause a stir in the wardrobe department. But she's not revealing any tantalising titbits about her *Strictly* outfits.

'I'm looking forward to wearing the dresses,' she says. 'I'm keen to wear what is suitable for me, and I am working together with the designers so I'm very happy. It's still a work in progress. But I will wear what is appropriate for the dance, and what I feel comfortable in.'

In fact, fashion is in her blood. Born in New York, to an American mother and Italian father, she moved to Italy when she was five and the family lived above a clothes shop. After studying law in Rome, she completed her master's degree at New York University. In 1990, she moved back to Italy and married millionaire lawyer Giancarlo Mazza, before setting up her own legal firm. Through her husband, a shareholder in Lazio football club, she met the club's manager Sven-Göran Eriksson in 1998. Two years later, Sven became England manager and the couple moved to London, launching Nancy into the limelight. They split in 2007 and she has since had a romance with theatre director Sir Trevor Nunn.

Although she was aware of *Strictly Come Dancing* before signing up, Nancy admits she hadn't watched the show. 'I knew about the programme and I know there is great excitement and fever around it,' she says. 'But I didn't watch it much because at the weekend I was usually traveling or going somewhere else. I prefer to have a virgin attitude towards *Strictly*.'

Although she's been asked before, Nancy felt that the time was right to devote herself to the series. 'This was the right moment,' she says. 'I chose the best year. It was a time that I could give myself a special break, and focus on something else, and I'm sure it's going to be quite challenging. I'm ready to get on with this big adventure. I hope I don't disappoint the whole country.'

The feisty Italian is no stranger to dance, having attended ballet classes as a child, but believes that will be little help on Saturday nights. 'I had my training in classic ballet but this is very different,' she says. 'I love to dance and I am a great dancer but here we are talking about a different kind of dance, a different mental challenge, because it is ballroom dancing and Latin dancing, so it's a new learning process. My training might help with my posture, but not with learning and perfecting these dances. Also *Strictly Come Dancing* is much more than just dancing.'

I'm ready to get on with this big adventure. I hope I don't disappoint the whole country

But the shapely star is enjoying training with partner Anton Du Beke, who is giving her plenty to laugh about. 'Anton is treating me very well,' she says. 'We get on well together and he has a lot of patience. He's not only a great dancer but a great teacher so I'm very happy with him. The great thing about Anton is his wonderful sense of humour, he's funny and that's something we have in common. I love his sense of humour, I hope he likes mine, and we're having a lot of fun. Sometimes it's better to laugh because it's not always easy.'

Russell Grant

Astrologer Russell Grant really will be 'dancing with the stars' when he takes to the *Strictly* dance floor but he's not getting much support from his celestial guides.

'To be honest with you, the stars say, "Don't do it. It's too much of a challenge,"' he admits. 'But people think the stars and astrology is all prediction when in fact it's about potential and choice, and I knew I was never going to get another chance to do this.'

Training with partner Flavia Cacace got off to a bad start when Russell suffered an agonising injury in the first week, perhaps demonstrating his heavenly advisors had a point.

'For the first few sessions, I was without my proper shoes and I was dancing in trainers so I pulled a tendon in the ball of my foot,' he explains. 'I had the chiropodist out, and I was using deep heat and support socks. I knew it was going to be a big challenge and I was right because I ended up with a badly bruised big toe, and also a sprain to the ball of my foot. At least it proves there's something in the stars!'

Even so, the Middlesex-born celeb is enjoying his time with partner Flavia. 'I adore the woman,' he says. 'She's my stage daughter and I'm her stage mother. That's the kind of relationship we have. She's wonderful. She's understanding. She's kind. In fact, I push myself too hard and she's the one telling me to take a break. Even with this bad foot I'm tending to forget about it because I'm so into the music and the dance.'

Russell, who turned 60 in February, began his career as an actor, appearing in numerous shows in London's West End. When not on stage, he practiced astrology as a hobby but, after being pictured giving a reading to the Queen Mother, in 1978, he was dubbed the 'Astrologer Royal' and became more famous for his horoscopes than his acting.

In recent years, he has suffered from bouts of ill health and before coming on the show, he shed ten stone in weight. But he admits his father was worried about his decision to take part. 'Mum is 84 now and she's delighted because it has always been her number one show,' he says. 'My dad was a bit sceptical to begin with, he was worried about my health because I had two heart scares earlier on in the decade and I was diagnosed with type two diabetes. Then, in April, I was directing *A Midsummer Night's Dream* and I fell off the stage and hurt my back and it turned into trochanteric bursitis, a painful hip condition, so I've been having injections into my hip. When I went for the medical, I didn't tell the doctor but she saw the bruise. I thought that was going to rule me out but I still passed.'

I have no idea how far I can go but I'd love to make it to Wembley because I'm a Middlesex boy

Russell is hoping his acting experience and sense of rhythm will be his secret weapons. And the twinkle-toed stargazer has already silenced those who assumed he has two left feet. 'Before we started, people were saying I would be the new Ann Widdecombe, the new John Sergeant, but because I showed a bit of rhythm, and did the sequence with Audley down the middle, that has all stopped. I think I'm a lot better than people anticipated.

'I have no idea how far I can go but I'd love to make it to Wembley because I'm a Middlesex boy. That would be a triumph but, however long I stay in, I would love to come out having learnt something.'

Strictly QUIZ

So you waltzed through the first show, and now the competition is getting tougher. Can you battle the nerves and dance your way into the grand final? Swap you dance shoes for thinking caps and see how if you can impress the judges.

1 **What was Ann and Anton's highest score in series 8?**

2 **Name the three professional dancers who have been partnering celebrities since the first series?**

3 **Who was the first celebrity to be awarded a perfect score of 40?**

4 **Which track did Kara and Artem perform their show dance to in the series 8 final?**

5 **Which newsman was first to be eliminated in series 4?**

6 **Who was Craig referring to in series 8's Hallowe'en show when he said, 'I wish it were that easy to make a man that looked like him.'?**

7 **Which duet did Alesha Dixon and Bruce Forsyth perform in the series 7 Grand Final?**

8 **Who did Bruce call 'Gavin Henson – the pocket version' after he stripped his jacket off at the end of his series 8 paso doble?**

9 **Which nervous celebrity gave up the ghost and stopped dancing halfway through his quarter-final foxtrot in series 5?**

10 **Who leads the live band on the show?**

11 **Which politician danced with Erin Boag in the 2010 Christmas special?**

12 **Who were the first celebrity couple to compete at the same time?**

13 **How did Mark Ramprakash and Karen Hardy make *Strictly* history during their salsa?**

14 **Who was the first sports personality on the *Strictly* dance floor?**

15 **Which leggy model was Ian Waite's partner in series 5?**

Round 2

DANCE OFF QUESTION:

Fourteen celebrities have also starred in *EastEnders*, before, during or after their *Strictly* stint. Can you name ten of them?

Under 5

Len says, 'You're getting on my nerves now. I know you can do it but you've got to put the work in if you want to get to the final.' Go to the dance off question to see if the public vote can save you.

Between 5 and 10

Alesha says; 'You've got the potential to be a winner. If you can get through to the final you have to pull out all the stops.'

You're in the dance off. Answer the question to go through.

Over 10

Craig, says 'A-ma-zing.' No dance off for you. You're straight through to the next round.

Answers 1. 21 for the Tango in week 4 2. Anton Du Beke, Erin Boag and Brendan Cole. 3. Jill Halfpenny for her series 2 jive. 4. Don't Stop Me Now 5. Nicholas Owen 6. Robin Windsor in his Frankenstein inspired Jive 7. Something's Gotta Give. 8. Vincent Simone 9. Matt Di Angelo 10. Dave Arch 11. Vince Cable 12. Gabby and Kenny Logan 13. Their microphones got tangled and they had to restart the dance. 14. Martin Offiah 15. Penny Lancaster-Stewart.

Dance off possible answers: Chris Parker, Jill Halfpenny, Patsy Palmer, Louisa Lytton, Letitia Dean, Matt Di Angelo, Phil Daniels, Gillian Taylforth, Zoe Lucker, Ricky Groves, Natalie Cassidy, Jimi Mistry, Scott Maslen, Kara Tointon

STRICTLY Style

Although she may be a fresh name to *Strictly* aficionados, new wardrobe designer Vicky Gill has long been a part of the backstage team. She has worked alongside previous designer Su Judd for five years and has stoned many a bodice in her long career. She's looking forward to the next season and promises more of the stunning outfits that add the signature sparkle to the show.

'The show's been running a long time and people have a great interest in the costumes, which is fabulous for us,' she says. 'Of all the shows you can watch on Saturday nights *Strictly* is massive in terms of costumes, so you can expect more good work this year.

'We will be working to put strong looks on the show, for the celebrities and professionals alike, so that we can keep up the standard and move it on. It's a wonderful show to work on, It's warm, it's fun, and it's very stylish and there's loads of variety for a costume designer.'

Having watched the show evolve, Vicky was thrilled with the new look and the themes that were introduced in series 8.

'It worked really well and helped to focus the show. It was quite exciting from a costume perspective because it allowed us to move away from the typical ballroom dress and have a little bit of fun.

'There were a lot more props last season and from the props to the music and choreography to the costumes we had somewhere to go. It's hard to keep everybody's attention so it certainly helps us to be able to key into different looks. Sometimes it was a bit mad and it may not be everybody's cup of tea, but it's Saturday night telly.'

Vicky and the team start working on initial ideas even before the competitors are announced and will liaise with the celebrities as soon as they are available. But as she explains, the majority of the work needs to be done at the last minute.

'Nine times out of ten, once they get into training, it's really tough for them,' she reveals. 'So the dresses are always very exciting in the beginning then training takes priority and we tend not to see them as often as we did, and they leave you to get on with it.

'We'll do an initial design three weeks before they are due to wear it. Then they'll come in the Friday of the week before – eight days before the relevant show – and that's when we'll really talk about it, and try to work out what's best for them and what they're comfortable with. After that we carry on and they fit their actual garment the Friday before the show.'

Stoning, alterations and adjustments often go up to the wire on Saturdays, with dresses even altered in length on the day. And as the couples take to the floor, the department waits with bated breath for any of the dreaded wardrobe malfunctions. Thankfully, the last series provided more magic than mayhem, and it is these moments that Vicky cherishes.

'For series 8, we had weeks when the sets, the choreography and the performance all gelled, you had some real magic moments. Whenever I think of my favourite dresses it is often because I enjoyed the entire piece and it all worked together.'

VICKY'S PICKS

Kara's American smooth – the Grand Final

Kara's final dress, for the American smooth, was the ultimate look for her. It was nude and peach and covered in crystals. I felt that she'd gone through the whole series, she looked great, she performed brilliantly, and that was the icing on the cake in terms of a look. It was beautiful and she looked like she'd arrived, she was a fully-fledged ballroom dancer, and she was allowed to wear the special dress. Kara had a lovely figure but it's not all about the figure. As you

go through the show the celebrities grow in confidence and performance and that in turn helps you to design dresses for them. We try to choose styles which will assist the performance generally, so a lot depends on personality. They could be beautiful and a size eight, and have it all going on, but if there's nothing else to draw from, it's quite difficult.

At the start, the nerves take hold and Kara's week 1 dress was very revealing, a little bit racy. To come out and perform in front of the nation, and have a very revealing frock, left her feeling a bit exposed. She looked great but it's more to do with their confidence than whether they like the dress or not. But Kara was brilliant all series, a lovely girl, really took the whole thing seriously in terms of learning but she still had a giggle, was quite light-hearted and she'd listen to our ideas and say, 'OK, let's do it!'

Patsy's cha cha cha dress – week 6

This outfit marked a turning point for Patsy. She was very nervous in terms of her age and she would always say to me, 'I don't want to be mutton …' To help, we tried to find style lines that were in line with fashion and trends so that she didn't feel too far out of her comfort zone. When we arrived at the beaded cha cha cha dress, it is very body-con and we wondered whether she would put it on. But she felt great by that point, and she said 'Come on, I've got to do this.' She'd lost a lot of weight and was much more confident in herself, and she rolled with it. Unfortunately, when Craig said she was 'cha cha chavvy' we all went, 'Oh no!' Her confidence had been peaking, she looked great, and we all died a little bit when we heard that. We thought, 'Now we're not going to get her in another frock like that.' But she looked and felt great and she went on to use that on the tour, so that was a definite turning point for her.

Felicity's foxtrot frock – week 2

Felicity had a number of elegant outfits and she was great to dress. At the beginning of the process, we like to try lots of things on the celebrities just to find out what silhouettes look good. As I do a variety of things through my work and I had the toile (a sample garment used in fittings before the actual dress is made) of a very well-known pop star, much younger than her, which Felicity got into, and she looked amazing. So we thought, "Go on Felicity!"

Felicity's foxtrot dress was one of the loveliest. It was a brown sheer dress with long sleeves and a silver band across the chest, and it was age-appropriate, she felt good in it and she looked great. She was a very attractive lady – and very flexible. I was there with an aching back and Felicity comes in and touches her toes in a nano-second!

Tina's Charleston dress – week 4

The feather dress Tina wore for the Charleston was great, from a fashion perspective, because it was quite cheeky and it wasn't the average fringed flapper dress, so out of all of hers that was my favourite. The feathers were sewed and glued on and then more were glued on to layer them up. From a design perspective it is like a couture garment, although a couture garment would have a lot more hand work in terms of stitching because it just wouldn't be feasible to produce all those dresses at that standard, so that's why a lot of them are glued.

Because she was ill one week, and went out reasonably early, Tina didn't have time to grow into her look. She started to look really good on the night she went out, when she did the Argentine tango. When we dressed her for the trailer, it was exciting because her outfit was quite extreme, with a big net skirt, and looked great.

Michelle's foxtrot frock – week 2

Another lovely girl, Michelle was very easy and worked well with my colleague Nicola, who dressed her on the show. The turquoise foxtrot dress was my favourite of hers. It was stoned at the top and floaty at the bottom, and up until that point they'd tried to give her a more pop feel so it was nice to see her in something so elegant. It suited her. We use a mixture of Swarovski crystals and stones from a company called Preciosa, so that one would have been a pretty expensive dress. Sometimes it's unbelievable how many crystals go on. There's 1440 stones in a ten gross packet, and you can use between four to ten packets for each dress. So sometimes the cost can be up to £900 for one dress. Obviously, not every dress can have that amount of crystals on it so we pick and choose the numbers but this dress did look amazing.

In one routine, Len criticised her high heels, because she is so tall. But their shoes stay with them for each dance. They get ballroom and Latin shoes at the beginning of the series and they normally have a two-and-a-half-inch heel, although sometimes, if the celebrity wants, it can be a three-inch heel. Michelle only had the standard heel but she is very tall. Once they have their shoes they don't want to part with them because they get comfortable as they wear them in. As the show progresses they start to look a little bit grubby and we try to change them, but very often they want to hold on to them. So we didn't feel bruised by Len's comments, we brushed that one off.

Ann Widdecombe's tango dress – week 4

When Ann came flying in to the dance floor, for her tango, she had a little fuchsia bolero jacket on and a black sparkly dress underneath. Once they'd done her hair and her make-up and she came in with the fuchsia and black outfit, I thought she looked really nice. Everyone also loved her Charleston dress, even though it's the longest one we've ever seen on the show.

Ann didn't want to be exposed in any way shape of form and that's fair enough. So she had her own guidelines of skirt length and fit, and she was very strong-willed. She knew what she wanted to do and what she wouldn't do. She was a very strong character who everybody grew to love in the end.

Strictly Spooky

On Hallowe'en, the series 8 couples took their routines to a whole new eerie level. Pamela and James took on a devilish look, Patsy became a mad scientist and Scott danced round a cauldron.

For the wardrobe department, the spooky special provided an exciting new challenge which could get all their creative juices flowing. Even though they were pre-warned, however, Vicky Gill and her team could have done with a crystal ball to help them get a head start.

'We knew it was coming at the beginning of the series and the production team have ideas about how they want it to run,' explains Vicky. 'But at that point we don't know what the contestants' capabilities are and it evolves as it goes on. So although we know it's coming, we can't design their dresses until we know how they're getting along.

'If someone is having a tough time, if they're not feeling good, it doesn't matter what dress we had in mind, we will change it for them. Also, they may choose a track which is better suited to their personality and their journey on *Strictly* rather than a track which they might have chosen in the summer when they joined the show. We can't start working on the outfits any more than three weeks before the night.

We have to hold fire and see how people are getting along and what their personalities are like first.'

For the wardrobe department, it's important to achieve the correct balance of playful fun and elegant style. While the couples enter into the spirit of a theme, they still want to go out on the floor looking good and feeling confident. And although the professionals and production team are bursting with ideas, it's Vicky's job to make sure the Hallowe'en special doesn't turn out to be a night of horrors.

'We go through everybody's ideas and wishes and we try to facilitate them while keeping a sense of style and elegance,' she says. 'For the Hallowe'en special it would be so easy to make it look like fancy dress and I don't think it did. There were some really nice costumes that week. You realised it was Hallowe'en but we weren't rushing down to the fancy dress shop hiring Dracula costumes!'

VICKY'S PICKS

Felicity and Vincent's cloaks and masks

The idea of the cloaks and masks for the Viennese waltz came from Vincent. If a prop like that is to be used, he will come to us and say 'This is what I want to choreograph into the dance. Can you make them?' And then we make it possible. When we know the concept we will design the dress around that feel. The thought behind Felicity's dress was that it should be quite plain at the front so that when the cloak came off, we were revealing a very detailed embellishment on the back. Felicity suited that style, she didn't need anything too over the top so we gave her chic style lines and concentrated on embellishments.

Jimi's 'Thriller' suit

I loved Jimi Mistry's 'Thriller' outfit, with the spooky contact lenses, and he was so excited about that dance. That was brilliant for the tour as well and obviously the viewers had enjoyed it, because as soon as he came out to do that paso doble on tour the audience went mad. Jimi was a really nice guy, and happy to enter into the spirit of everything, so that was a memorable outfit for me. The men tend to leave us to get on with it. The ladies, in Jimi's case Flavia, will come up with some suggestions of how they'd like it to be and production might have something different in mind so we'll try and bring it together. Most of the professionals have been part of the team for quite a long time, so they feel quite confident in the costume department and they know that everybody is trying hard to deliver.

Kara and Artem's *Phantom of the Opera*

When someone requests a specific prop, such as the *Phantom of the Opera* mask for Kara and Artem's paso doble, we find it or make it, depending on time, money and what garments we actually have to make because they're not available elsewhere. It's all about juggling man hours and finding the best solution to what we need to achieve that week so it all depends on how big the week is, how many hands we have on board to glue and stick.

That mask was bought and that was quite an easy theme to convey, because as soon as the music's started the audience have got it.

Movie Magic

A touch of Hollywood glamour added a sprinkling of stardust to the *Strictly* studio for the quarter-finals. An opening *Star Wars* sequence was followed by the professionals own tribute to the silver screen, as Robin and Kristina kicked off with a *Grease* tribute, James and Ola danced a *Top Gun* routine, Artem and Katya emulated John Travolta and Uma Thurman in *Pulp Fiction* and Anton and Erin became 'A Couple of Swells' for an *Easter Parade* dance.

Style-wise we saw Scott Maslen make a magnificent James Bond, opposite scantily-clad Ursula Andress lookalike Natalie, Gavin and Katya becoming *The Blues Brothers* and Kara taking on the Argentine tango, *Moulin Rouge* style. In her tribute to *Ghost*, Pamela looking every inch the screen goddess in a white ball gown which had Alesha gasping 'You looked like a Hollywood star. These are the moments I look forward to on *Strictly*, when you get the perfect song, the perfect dress, the perfect choreography and perfectly danced.'

Designer Vicky Gill had a similar moment while watching Anton and Erin as the show kicked off.

'The dresses really fit Hollywood week, because it goes hand in hand with the style of ballroom, and that was certainly the case with Anton and Erin. For the new series there had been Hallowe'en and plenty of different props, and watching Anton and Erin's *Easter Parade* routine I just thought, "Isn't that lovely."'

VICKY'S PICKS

Matt and Aliona's *Austin Powers* tribute

The Austin Powers costumes were among my favourites for the whole series. I loved Matt's costume because it was fun, from a viewer's perspective and we had great fun designing Aliona's dress. It was actually a dress that we'd used for a photo-shoot prior to *Strictly* so we customised it to fit Aliona and work for that piece, and it turned out really well.

Kara's *Moulin Rouge* look

That was quite powerful. We've mentioned the dances where the whole thing comes together from the set, to the choreography, to the frock, there was a moment of magic here. It was beautiful to watch.

Pamela's *Ghost* dress

The Viennese waltz dress was a triumph because you would imagine that having a white dress might not work for someone of Pamela's age but she looked beautiful. She looked fantastic and she was fantastic so hats off to Pamela!

On tour she was amazing yet again, and you wonder how she does it. You have Kara on one side – the young, beautiful, very capable dancer – and then Pamela, from an age perspective at least, on the other side, but equally appealing.

Pamela's body shape changed a lot. We create stands, or tailor's dummies, at the beginning of the series which reflect their natural body shape and as we go through the show the shape of the stands are all altered. Most of the celebrities have fitness regimes outside of *Strictly*, whether it is the gym or running, but as soon as they start dancing they can't believe the difference. Patsy couldn't believe how much her body shape changed and Pamela, especially, looked great and felt great.

The battle for the trophy is about to end, but the competition is hotter than ever. Can you make it through the toughest challenge and emerge triumphant to lift that glitterball? Or will it be murder on the dance floor?

1 Name the third GMTV presenter to take to the *Strictly* Dance Floor.

2 In which dance would you be most likely to see a fleckerl?

3 Which two dances were introduced for the first time in series 4?

4 Which professional dancer became to the first winner to make it through to the following year's final?

5 Which judge told series 6 winner Tom Chambers, after his showdance, 'You're like Bisto gravy, darling – you saved the best 'til last!

6 What percentage of the American smooth should be in hold?

7 Who did Len describe as 'two lovely dancing hobbits' ?

8 Last year Kara and Artem scored 39 for their rumba. Name the only other couple to match that score.

9 Who was the first celebrity to get a 1 from Craig?

10 Which celebrity from Blackpool was knocked out in his home town?

11 Which dance, according to Len, is about a gaucho coming off the pampas and approaching a lady of the night?

12 Whose Spanish dancing had Bruno declaring, 'Dad's Army does the paso' ?

13 Which professional partnered Zoe Ball in series 3?

14 Specialists Chris Marques and Jaclyn Spencer are often called in to help couples master which dance?

15 Who was guest judge on series 7 of the show?

Now add up you scores and await the judges' final verdict.

Round 3
The Grand Final

Under 5
Alesha says, 'Sorry but you don't deserve to be in the final. The honeymoon's over for me.' You have danced your last dance.

Between 5 and 10
Len says, 'You came out here with plenty of vim and vigour but you lost it a little bit along the way. All in all though, a good job.'

Over 10
Craig says, 'One word. Fab-u-lous'. Bruno adds, 'You *Strictly* star you! You gave it your all and tonight you were inbeatable.'

Congratulations, **the glitterball is YOURS**

Answers 1. Andrew Castle 2. Viennese Waltz 3. Salsa, Argentine Tango 4. Lilia Kopylova 5. Craig Revel Horwood 6. 40% 7. Chris Hollins and Ola Jordan 8. Rachel Stevens and Vincent Simone 9. Quentin Willson (series two) 10. Craig Kelly 11. Argentine tango 12. John Sergeant 13. Ian Waite 14. Salsa 15. Darcey Bussell

Strictly CROSSWORD

Across

5 Name shared by Phil, who went out in week 1 in 2009, and Paul, who left in week 2 in 2010 (7)
7 - - - Lowe, Australian dancer who helped Scott progress to the semis in 2010 (7)
10 & **16A** Former *Blue Peter* presenter who finished runner-up in series 8 (4,5)
11 Heather - - -, singer who reached week 8 with Brian in 2008 (5)
12 - - - Boag, the only female dancer to have competed in every series (4)
13 Lithuanian dancer who got Gavin to take his shirt off in series 8 (5)
16 See 10A
18 First named shared by two goalkeepers who competed in 2006 and 2010 (5)
20 - - - Palmer, *EastEnders* star who made it to week 8 with Anton (5)
24 - - - Morley, Miss World founder who created the *Come Dancing* show for the BBC in 1949 (4)
26 Middle name of the first judge to give his marks (5)
27 One of the pair who tells us every week to keep dancing (4)
29 Louisa - - -, actress who, at 17, remains the youngest competitor to appear on the show (6)
30 Dancer who was *Strictly*'s first ever winner (7)

Down

1 Former *EastEnders* actress who beat 10A and Pamela in the final last year (4)
2 See 4D
3 - - - Rouass, actress who gave Anton his best result so far making it to week 12 in 2009 (5)
4 & **2D** Flavia's partner last year who achieved their highest score of 32 the week they were eliminated (4,6)
6 - - - Snowdon, model who partnered 30A in 2008 (4)
8 Winner of series 5 who became a judge in series 7 (6)
9 - - - Waite, dancer who has appeared in 7 out of 8 series (3)
14 Russian-born dancer who won in his first year partnering 1D (5)
15 Denise - - -, athlete who was runner-up with 9D in series 2 (5)
17 Actress who formed half of Team Kendal Vince Cake in series 8 (8)
19 - - - Hingis, tennis player who may be the best dancer to have gone out in week 1 (7)
21 Flamboyant judge who gives marks on both sides of the Atlantic (5)
22 - - - Pollard, journalist who's the mother of *It Takes Two*'s Claudia (3)
23 Julian - - -, comedian who finished third with 12A in series 2 (5)
25 - - - Fearon, former *Corrie* star who was Camilla's partner in series 4 (3)
28 'Wishing On A - - -', Rose Royce song to which Scott and 7A did a rumba (4)

Strictly DANCES WORDSEARCH

I	F	B	C	S	W	I	N	G	N	I	L	U	A	P
O	S	B	I	P	O	H	Y	D	N	I	L	M	E	E
T	E	J	S	H	O	W	D	A	N	C	E	A	E	T
O	N	N	V	I	B	R	O	C	M	R	B	F	C	S
R	L	O	W	B	U	E	H	Z	I	S	E	R	L	K
T	M	D	T	M	A	A	V	C	D	L	S	E	A	C
X	E	O	B	S	C	R	A	I	B	I	E	E	T	I
O	A	A	O	H	E	N	O	O	J	U	N	S	I	U
F	S	B	A	R	S	L	D	C	L	T	J	T	N	Q
U	D	C	M	M	L	O	R	O	K	L	B	Y	J	A
R	H	O	O	A	S	L	G	A	S	N	E	L	L	M
A	W	O	W	A	S	N	A	B	H	S	R	E	S	E
W	T	Y	P	N	A	O	H	B	G	C	A	O	N	D
H	R	U	S	T	C	D	E	A	S	L	A	S	L	O
Z	T	L	A	W	E	S	E	N	N	E	I	V	H	L

AMERICAN SMOOTH
BALLROOM
CHA CHA CHA
CHARLESTON
FOXTROT
FREESTYLE
JIVE
LATIN
LINDYHOP
PASO DOBLE
QUICKSTEP
ROCK 'N' ROLL
RUMBA
SALSA
SAMBA
SHOWDANCE
SWING
TANGO
VIENNESE WALTZ

Strictly**Stats**

Ever wondered exactly how many hours a celebrity couple trained? Or how many bottles of fake tan are used every series? For all the number crunchers out there, we've put together some fascinating facts, figures and league tables to add to your in depth knowledge of all things *Strictly*.

Hours of Pain

Despite their triumph in series 8, Kara and Artem weren't the couple who spent the most time in the training room. In fact, they managed nearly forty hours less than hard-working duo Pamela and James.

Series 8 training hours

Pamela and James – 267 hours
Matt and Aliona – 238 hours
Kara and Artem – 228.5 hours

Fun Fact

Series 8 saw the celebs and dancers slap on an amazing 40 litres, or four gallons, of fake tan. They also sparkled their way through through over 120 cans of body glitter.

The Perfect Ten

As every celeb hits the dance floor, they are hoping to get a glimpse of that elusive '10' paddle from one or all of the judges. But it's not always the couple with the most perfect scores who leave with the trophy, as the league table of tens below shows. The top two were pipped at the post in the final and only three *Strictly* champs made it into the top ten.

Celebrity	Number of 10s	Number of dances scoring 10
Ricky Whittle	28	10
Rachel Stevens	25	9
Kara Tointon	21	9
Lisa Snowdon	20	7
Alesha Dixon	19	9
Pamela Stephenson	17	6
Ali Bastian	12	4
Matt Di Angelo	9	3
Austin Healey	8	5
Mark Ramprakash	7	2

Perfect Professionals

Despite only dancing in two series Natalie Lowe tops the table for the most tens when it comes to the professional dancers. Here is the league table for the top ten dancers.

Total Tens	
Natalie Lowe	34
Vincent Simone	26
Brendan Cole	22
Artem Chigvintsev	21
Matthew Cutler	19
James Jordan	17
Camilla Dallerup	13
Erin Boag	13
Brian Fortuna	12
Flavia Cacace	9

Judging the Judges

Since the start of *Strictly* the judges have awarded a total of 229 perfect scores. Bruno has proved the most generous on the panel, although Alesha is fast catching up. Here's how the judges scored.

Bruno	76
Len	59
Alesha	35
Arlene	33
Craig	19
Darcey (guest judge)	6

The Dreaded One

The '1' paddle has only reared its ugly head eight times in all eight series – and seven of those were Craig's. The other was awarded by Arlene for Quentin Willson's series 2 cha cha cha.

Unsurprisingly, Ann and Anton were the most frequent recipients of this damning score.

The league of shame is as follows:

Ann Widdecombe and Anton Du Beke – series 8 rumba, salsa and samba
Quentin Willson and Hazel Newbury – series 2 cha cha cha (2 x 1)
Fiona Phillips and Brendan Cole – series 3 rumba
Gary Rhodes and Karen Hardy – series 6 cha cha
John Sergeant and Kristina Rihanoff – series 6 cha cha cha

Average Scores

Although she can't claim the most perfect scores series 5 champ and current *Strictly* judge Alesha has the highest average score of any contestant – a whopping 36.5. The lowest is Quentin Willson, scoring eight points for his single dance in series 2. Here's the top ten.

	No of dances	Total points	Average
Alesha Dixon	16	584	36.5
Ricky Whittle	19	757	35.8
Rachel Stevens	16	573	35.8
Kara Tointon	16	571	35.7
Pamela Stephenson	14	491	35.1
Zoe Ball	13	454	34.9
Lisa Snowdon	16	557	34.8
Tom Chambers	16	552	34.5
Austin Healey	12	414	34.5
Matt Baker	16	548	34.3

Top of the Props

With swings, window boxes and even a front door, *Strictly* series eight really went to town on the props. Doctor Pamela donned a white coat, Patsy became a mad scientist, complete with bubbling potions and test tubes, and Scott danced round a cauldron. But it was Matt and Aliona who claim to have got the ball rolling with their very first cha cha cha.

'In the first couple of weeks we started the prop war,' said Matt. 'They've got wellies and a rucksack – and binoculars! It's nice to be a trendsetter as opposed to a trend follower.'

Crystal-studded laptops, chairs, tables and hat-stands followed, and by the time Anton and Ann performed their *Titanic* rumba in week 9 the set dressing had progressed to a ship's bell, fake fog and a whopping great iceberg. For the production crew, who have seconds to prepare the set for the next dance, the innovation provides a new challenge and one that they rose to admirably. But it also fell to wardrobe to provide the extras.

'The props are shared between costume and production, and everyone works together, depending on what everyone has got to do,' reveals wardrobe designer Vicky Gill. 'For instance, Matt's flat cap came from us but the binoculars would come through props. If it's worn, that's our responsibility but that's an example of a grey area. We have a shopping list of what's got to be done and we go through it and say, "Are we taking that or knocking it back over the net?" So, if we want to, we can send it back to props and have a little giggle about it.'

Although he's usually a stickler for tradition, Len feels that props can have their place but he warns that they can also add complications. 'You can practise your routine and get that nailed as best you can, but the thing that's always going to be the possible stumbling block is the props – getting a ring out of your pocket and that sort of malarkey – so they do take a bit of a chance sometimes.

'My feeling now is that if the props are not overly used, and it doesn't get in the way too much of the dancing, then have a go. I'd rather that than what you get sometimes when they faff about up on the stage for ages at the start, then do about 20 seconds of dancing and then faff about again.'

Italian judge Bruno Tonioli is used to seeing props on the American version of the show, *Dancing with the Stars,* and believes they make the show more interesting. 'It's not a straight ballroom competition,' he insists. 'If you want that you go to Blackpool. We have to entertain and our show has to reach the widest

Len loved the use of the door and suitcase in Scott's jive to 'Hit the Road Jack'. 'Scott and Natalie's jive was great entertainment,' he says. 'I'm not a great lover of the doors and all that, but I must say it was entertaining.'

Craig's favourite use of props was when Aliona sat on a swing under a rose-covered arch to begin her Viennese waltz with Matt. 'I liked the swing,' he says. 'That was a nice little touch.' But Len wasn't so impressed on the night, joking, 'I was bit concerned about the start. I thought Alan Titchmarsh was about to pop out.'

possible audience, while keeping within the rules of the show. You still have to make it entertaining so those extra bits really add to the entertainment part of the show and sometimes it works, sometimes it gives a comic spin, but it's another dimension that I think the public really enjoys.'

Surprisingly, theatre choreographer Craig was the least keen on the dramatic device to start with.

'At the beginning I wasn't a fan of the props and then they grew on me, and I think they do add a dimension because they set up the dancers with a story,' he reveals. 'It's good for the people at home to know that dance isn't just a sport, that it does have artistic interpretation and ability and flair. Having props helped support the storyline and gives an indication of what the dance is about, rather than it just being about technique.'

Jimi and Flavia used two windows on stage to play amorous neighbours in their week 4 Charleston. While Craig and Alesha loved the story-telling, Len wasn't keen on the props and Bruno commented, 'I was a bit worried at the beginning because I wasn't sure if I was watching Wisteria Lane or the Tardis, but once you got going, you really went into character.'

Paul Daniels produced lovely assistant Ola from his magic box in his week 1 cha cha cha but failed to cast a spell on the judges. 'The best part of that routine was the empty box,' said Craig.

Ringmaster Matt made an impressive entrance on a unicycle during his Charleston. 'I did enjoy the Charleston,and especially the unicycling,' he says. 'I'd done that when I was a boy but not since. It was hilarious – it was all like a trip back to my boyhood.'

Debonair Brendan slid down the banister in his week 2 foxtrot as Michelle waited demurely on a park bench. 'I liked the bench,' said Len. 'It just seemed you were a long time before you got off of it.'

Pamela and James took internet dating to a whole new level as they kicked off their cha cha cha in bowler hats and suits, tapping away on sparkling stoned laptops. Bruno gushed, 'Just met on the net and all the clothes come off, promising delight!'

Chairs were a favourite prop among the celebs and not always for the right reasons. After suffering a painful foot injury in week 9, Patsy remarked, 'Luckily the routine this week has a chair in it. I'm hoping to have a nice little sit for 16 bars.'
But Kara made better use of the furniture when she flipped it over in the midst of her week 10 tango. Bruno got so excited he leapt up and told her, 'Spectacular, spectacular. A tango that was theatrical magic' before falling off his own seat!

SOLUTIONS *Strictly* CROSSWORD AND DANCES WORDSEARCH

Across: 5 Daniels, 7 Natalie, 10 Matt, 11 Small, 12 Erin, 13 Katya, 16 Baker, 18 Peter, 20 Patsy, 24 Eric, 26 Revel, 27 Tess, 29 Lytton, 30 Brendan.

Down: 1 Kara, 2 Mistry, 3 Laila, 4 Jimi, 6 Lisa, 8 Alesha, 9 Ian, 14 Artem, 15 Lewis, 17 Felicity, 19 Martina, 21 Bruno, 22 Eve, 23 Clary, 25 Ray, 28 Star.

AMERICAN SMOOTH
BALLROOM
CHA CHA CHA
CHARLESTON
FOXTROT
FREESTYLE
JIVE
LATIN
LINDYHOP
PASO DOBLE
QUICKSTEP
ROCK 'N' ROLL
RUMBA
SALSA
SAMBA
SHOWDANCE
SWING
TANGO
VIENNESE WALTZ

I F B C S W I N G N I L U A P
O S B I P O H Y D N I L M E E
T E J S H O W D A N C E A E T
O N N V I B R O C M R B F C S
R L O W B U E H Z I S E R L K
T M D T M A A V C D L S E A C
X E O B S C R A I B I E E T I
O A A O H E N O O J U N S I U
F S B A R S L D C L T J T N Q
U D C M M L O R O K L B Y J A
R H O O A S L G A S N E L L M
A W O W A S N A B H S R E S E
W T Y P N A O H B G C A O N D
H R U S T C D E A S L A S L O
Z T L A W E S E N N E I V H L

This book is published to accompany the television series entitled *Strictly Come Dancing*, first broadcast on BBC1 in 2011.

Executive Producer: Moira Ross
Series Producers: Liz Trott and Ed Booth

10 9 8 7 6 5 4 3 2 1

Published in 2011 by BBC Books, an imprint of Ebury Publishing.
A Random House Group Company

BBC Books would like to thank Moria Ross, Clodagh O' Donoghue, Kirsty Bysouth, Claire Bridgland, Kim Winston, Rory Dalziel, Richard Curwen, Jagdeep Sharma, Richard Halliwell, Elizabeth Gray and the rest of the *Strictly Come Dancing* Production team.

Text by Alison Maloney
Introductions by Sir Bruce Forsyth and Tess Daly

The Random House Group Limited Reg. No. 954009

Addresses for companies within the Random House Group can be found at www.randomhouse.co.uk

A CIP catalogue record for this book is available from the British Library.

ISBN 978 1 849 90155 0

The Random House Group Limited supports the Forest Stewardship Council® (FSC®), the leading international forest certification organisation. All our titles that are printed on Greenpeace approved FSC® certified paper carry the FSC® logo. Our paper procurement policy can be found at www.randomhouse.co.uk/environment

Commissioning editor: Lorna Russell
Project editor: Laura Higginson
Design and illustrations: Bobby&Co
Food photography by Craig Robertson © Woodlands Books Ltd 2011; Series 8 photography by Guy Levy © BBC 2011, Series 9 photography by Guy Levy and Jon Cottam © BBC 2011; Live Tour photography © Alfie Hitchcock; *Dance Class* step illustrations © Bobby&Co; *Dance Class* hold illustrations © Mike Garland; all other photography © iStockphoto.com and Fotolia.
Recipes by: Sarah Cook
Food Stylist: Rosie Reynolds
Props Stylist: Cynthia Nixon
Production: Antony Heller

Colour origination by: Altaimage, London
Printed and bound in Germany by Mohn Media GmbH

To buy books by your favourite authors and register for offers, visit www.randomhouse.co.uk